IN DEEP

Also by Maxine Kumin

IN DEEP
Country Essays

BY

MAXINE KUMIN

Beacon Press   Boston

Beacon Press
25 Beacon Street
Boston, Massachusetts 02108

Beacon Press books
are published under the auspices of
the Unitarian Universalist Association of Congregations.

95 94 93 92 91 90 89   8 7 6 5 4 3 2

Text design by Camilla Filancia

"Life on a Hill," "The Mushroom Hunt," "The Family Saddle Horse," "Building Fence," "Two Foals" (as "Spring Journal: Two Foals"), "The Country Kitchen," "Scotch Highlanders," and "Popple" first appeared in *Country Journal;* "Herons" (as "Blue Herons") in *Harvard* magazine; " 'Silver Snaffles' " (as "Why Is It That Girls Love Horses?") in *Ms.* magazine; "Getting into the Register" in *Upcountry* magazine; "The Poet and the Mule" in *Ontario Review;* and "The Unhand-selled Globe" in *Harper's.*
Grateful acknowledgment is made for permission to reprint the following copyrighted material: "Bringing Up Boomerang," "Estivating," "Wintering Over," and "Journal—Late Winter—Spring 1978" from *To Make a Prairie: Essays on Poets, Poetry, and Country Living* by Maxine Kumin. Copyright © 1979 by the University of Michigan. Used by permission of the University of Michigan Press.
An excerpt from *The Reivers* by William Faulkner. Copyright © 1962 by William Faulkner. By permission of Random House, Inc.

Library of Congress Cataloging-in-Publication Data
Kumin, Maxine
    In deep.
    Essays previously published in various magazines and in her To make a prairie.
    1. Country life.   I. Title
[PS3521.U6381S 1988]   814'.54 ·   87-72730
ISBN 0-8070-6323-1

Dedication

For VICTOR, who proclaims
that we are "in *too* deep,"
but somehow manages to keep the pump running,
the fences in reasonable repair,
mice from the root cellar,
creosote out of the chimneys,
and never quite relinquishes
his saving sense of humor.

Contents

[vii]

CONTENTS

IN DEEP

In Deep

Early winter. Foliage gone, the woods reveal their inner architecture. In a strong wind, oak and maple branches creak and rub against each other, cranky as old door hinges. I can see in deep now, deep into this second-growth forest where pastures once were, and farms prospered. I can spot the occasional apple tree and lilac sprawl, the tumbled stone walls and caved-in foundations at a considerable distance.

The deerflies, those scourges of midsummer shaped like tiny deltoid planes, have vanished. Ground wasps that lurked in rotten logs waiting to pounce on the unwary traveler are now in hibernation. Only the deer hunters are left for us to contend with.

Weekends we ride out in threes and fours, horses and people bedecked in extremely orange pinnies—Ten Mile Cloth, the manufacturer calls it, claiming it can be seen at that remove. Each of us has a cowbell tied to one stirrup. I carry a folding saw across the cantle of my saddle. Aurally and visually we make a fearsome procession. Of course the hunters hate us, but these are *our* woods too, and this is our only season for bushwhacking.

Midweek, theorizing that the Sunday shooters have gone home, I risk my neck alone. Riding along old rangeways between vanished settlements I peer down every track. All those roads not taken! Bending low under overhanging branches, sometimes stopping to saw my way clear, I take them one by one. And one by one they peter out like rambling thoughts, glimmering ideas unrealized.

Somehow I am never cured of my fantasy; surely one will carry me through? One day, riding in deep, the perfect trail will materialize, a leafy carpet underfoot, and overhead just room enough—a tunnel for my chestnut horse and me. We will trot for miles this way, admiring the crackle we make in late November, admiring the configurations of hummocks and rivulets underfoot with glistens of ice between, and bits of bright blue sky visible over the next rise. Eventually we will come out on the other side.

What is waiting on the other side? Maybe nothing special, maybe only more of the same, dear enough for this watcher. But the quest is real. To get there you have to go in deep.

Life on a Hill

"How's your hill?" guests invited to dinner used to inquire.

"Fine. The sanding truck was just here," we would gloat (sometimes). Or (occasionally) when freshly plowed out, "Terrific! Much better than it is all summer." For in summer, although passable, the road turns to bone- and axle-jarring corduroy. Mufflers drop off. Gaskets loosen. Dust clouds fly about like dervishes.

More often, particularly in mud season, the answer would be equivocal.

"Depends. You have four-wheel drive? Oh, you'll make it, just come up fast, easy on the turns, and pull in to the right."

Or: "You don't? But you have three hundred pounds of grain over the rear wheels? Well, you can give it a try. Start from across the wooden bridge at the bottom so you can get a good running jump. You'll have to slow down some on that tricky little curve, but if you get past that, gun it hard up the straight part. You'll need everything you've got to make it to the top."

Some years ago, wearying of this intricate initiation of visitors, we scooped out a parking space down by the infamous "tricky little curve." Three-tenths of a mile uphill from our mailbox on the road, that bend is so nefarious that neophytes often skidded into a snowbank or wound up fender-deep in mud there. It's only another tenth of a mile uphill to the house from that elbow, though. After dinner, using the old aggie truck, a '67 Dodge Power Wagon of prodigious gifts and fearsome proportions, we pushed or pulled the hapless guests out of jams.

Actually, the top is not the top, to paraphrase Gertrude Stein. It is merely the wrist bone in this giant arm of hill. Another, broader plateau exists a little farther uphill, some fifty yards above house and barn. There, on an almost flat grassy sward, the vegetable garden flourishes. Beyond the garden, a saucer pond. And just beyond the pond, on our only truly, though briefly, level piece of earth, our riding ring.

The first settlers in this part of New England divided themselves according to economics and temperament much as they had in the Old Country. The thrifty, practiced farmers squatted along the riverbottom land and got on with their crops. The well-to-do settlers sought out the tops of hills, where admirable views were to be had, and built imposing structures out of the native pine. A hundred years ago the biggest house atop the tallest hill in any town, up and down the Merrimack River, was invariably the mill owner's house. And then the modest in-betweeners, those without resources for the land highest up or the richest bottom land, snugged homesteads into the crook of a hill, facing southeast, out of the prevailing wind. They struggled to clear the gentler peaks and valleys of their hills, as well as the occasional plateaus formed by the glaciers. Some of the homesteaders lasted, grazing cows or sheep on the thin topsoil, until World War II.

Those of us who now inhabit these hillside farms alternately bless and curse the first comers. We bless them for having the wisdom to build out of the wind. On a February day when the thermometer barely creeps up to zero and the wind-chill factor is a terrifying minus forty, our bay mares stand blissfully sunbathing in the lee of the barn. Across the road, sheltered by a fortuitous dip in the land, the heifers have folded their legs in on the snow for a midday nap.

But there's no view of the river valley below. The front of the house looks southeast across the road to the barn; the barn smiles onto a tilt-table pasture. Beyond the pasture, hills, and higher hills. The sun drops below the rim at three o'clock in winter. By four, lengthening shadows bring all the livestock back to the starting gate. Animals fed, watered, bedded down, a preprandial depression skulks in by five.

How do you build a barn on a hill? They did it putting practicality foremost, with a cavernous opening—a giant pit for the cow manure—facing downhill. Warmth coming off the pile may or may not have reached the first floor. Certainly the redolence did. Twenty years ago, we redid the barn's foundations and built stalls into the earthworks. The north and west walls are solid concrete, dungeon-damp and sure. The third wall, which follows the contour of a gentle downslope, allows for two stall windows facing south. The front, reinforced concrete below grade, stands open to morning sun or easterly drizzle. It can be closed with two mammoth sliding doors. In our innocence, we used to snug these elaborate panels shut on cold winter nights, but snow melting off the roof at sundown all too often dripped along their length and, as the temperature fell, soldered them tight by morning. If I forgot to leave the pickaxe propped outside, I frequently had to burgle my way into the barn via a stall window. A startled mare once took violent exception to my forced entry. Now we routinely leave the doors ajar. With several equines breathing inside, things are cozy enough.

No matter what ploys we resort to, however, in the spring runoff, the barn fills. First a trickle, then twelve rivulets. Then a flood. We ditch, underdrain, build ramparts of sawdust and manure, mutter annual imprecations. By May, all is habitable and forgiven. The first farmers, of course, knew all this. They kept their beasts upstairs. Their cows calved, their mares foaled in dry stalls, albeit on hard boards, probably bedded none too thickly with homegrown straw.

But in spring, time for tapping maple trees, the hill is a benevolence. Purple tubing threads its way downslope in great serpentines. We need only watch and listen to the silence as gravity does the work. No more tedious lifting and emptying of buckets. No more gently arrhythmic plinkings of sap droplets into buckets, either. Sixty trees drip their bounty into the plastic life lines. A stream of sugar water flows into the collecting vat.

Trudging uphill to check the garish lines of tubing for sags, I think, "Anything might be born in this still time, in the punky snow." Friends of ours had a slumberous bear in a hollow ash tree in their sugarbush last spring. We paid the bear a visit. It twitched and breathed and went on with its hibernation. Cubs are born, generally two to a litter, in late January or February, says the *Field Guide to American Wildlife*. I think of Jim Wright's poem in which as the bear "lay asleep, her cubs fell / Out of her hair, / And she did not know them."

In the fall, when riverbottom gardens are swathed ghost-like in sheets, drop cloths, and a season's worth of Sunday papers, our garden may have several more frost-free nights. Zucchini may wither and blacken below. Up here it is still putting out new little pencils. Still picking tomatoes and cukes and Kentucky Wonders, we have won as much as a two-week reprieve beyond the frost kill of the lowlands.

Three or four halcyon days in winter, when a new snow-fall smooths the contours of our hill and cushions its sides where earlier snowbanks have hardened to icy crusts, we can ski down on cross-country skis without fear of fracture. Those same few days I long for a sleigh. Even though the slow raspings of the plow in the night are the most luxuriously welcome sounds of our hill lives, this incurable romantic wishes for a few days' respite from the world. If the plow breaks down, if Harry the operator catches the flu, if the sanding truck pops a gasket—snowbound! By sleigh I could circumnavigate the town.

When the melt begins and house and barn stand apart like Noah's ark, all of us awash on a sea of mud, I try to plan ahead, to have groceries and grain on hand for the inevitable few days when the road is all but impassable.

Farming on the slant, liming and fertilizing fourteen acres of forage fields, requires ingenuity and courage. You can do a lot of things with a walk-behind tractor, but fortunately one thing you're not likely to do is tip over on the slope. A horse-drawn spreader can also with impunity tack east and west across the hill at a sedate plod. The driver will have walked two miles per acre in intimate contact with the contours of the field. But during that week of fertilizing the fields, from the top line of those three back pastures, the view to the north is spectacular. Hilltop sitters have it on a daily basis. Here it is more precious because seldom seen: the town below like a toy set for Lionel trains, the glimpse of Kearsarge beyond, a perfect papier-mâché mountain. On the opposite ridge, the fine white farmhouses of an earlier century, well kept and gleaming as though freshly waxed.

Clearing land on the slope or simply cutting hillside trees to keep the woodlot thinned raises other difficulties. Granted, the angle can work to a woodcutter's benefit if the big oak's fall is correctly plotted. But the danger of error is enhanced, too. No margin for misstep when you must stand braced against the hill while making the second sawcut that will send forty feet of tree crashing through the forest canopy. On the other hand, bringing wood out of the lot can sometimes be a matter of a few judicious tugs and several free revolutions. No doubt the wheel was born somewhere on a primal slope.

Fencing up- and downhill is several times more arduous than running three lines of boards on the level. What the little bubble inside the carpenter's tool says may run counter to the eye of the distant beholder. Bringing those two judgments into harmony requires continual fudging of measurements and compromise of position as the hemlock lengths are hammered in place. And oh! the wrong angles at which boards are occasionally cut, the botching and mismatchings. Is the field sweeter when the fence is finished? Possibly a straightaway fence wouldn't please the eye as much.

The camaraderie of other halfway-hill people adds considerable relish to this chosen way of life. You'd be surprised how many of us there are, hidden in the pleats and folds of hills neither massive enough to have attracted the ski industry nor tame enough for paved roads and subdivisions. We have traded easy access for solitary splendor. In a sense, we live on an island, at the mercy of wind and tides, or at least of ice and mud. All of us are parts of the main, however, as John Donne pointed out. But put it in four-wheel drive before you come up to join us.

SPRING

The Mushroom Hunt

Take a rainy morning in late April or May, preferably the third or fourth wet one in a row. The oak leaves have reached thumbnail size, the shadberry has come into bloom, the *plunk-plunk* of a determined small rain is creating an almost unbearable indoor tension. It is a day to put your head into the poncho hood, hang a flat-bottomed basket over your arm, and sally forth, eyes on the ground, on a leisurely ramble.

"The world of wonder at your feet"—so goes the motto of the North American Mycological Society—awaits you. Will there, won't there be morels? Possibly some fresh chicken-of-the-woods lurks on an old tree stump. Even though the calendar decrees it's too soon for puffballs, you'll want to look closely along the pond dam, where they pop up annually like miniature golfballs.

For wherever there is sufficient moisture in the earth or air, accompanied by temperatures congenial to growth, fungi, lowly plantlike organisms from which the green pigment chlorophyll is absent, appear. Many fungi produce large fruiting forms, and these include not only the familiar gilled mushroom with its undersurface decorated with thin, spokelike structures radiating from the stem, but related and easier-to-identify non-gilled growths of meadow and forest. With these the beginner need not suffer any identity crises. The morels, puffballs, chanterelles, teeth fungi, boletes, corals, and polypores mentioned in this essay represent a mere smattering of the more than six hundred known edible species that fruit in the United States.

All told, more than three thousand different species of mushroom fungi occur in this country. All of them reproduce by means of spores, little one-celled particles contained on the mushroom's gills—if it has gills—or on its tubes, pores, teeth—if it has any of these—or, in the case of the sophisticated puffball, within its round, fruiting body.

Loosely, spores are to fungi as seeds to garden plants. The sex life of the fungus, however, is somewhat more complicated than it would appear. A spore may lie dormant for as long as six years. When it germinates, a primary mycelium is produced, which, in most instances, must then ferret out and join with a mycelium of the opposite gender to send up secondary mycelia capable of bearing fruit. The white thread-like material often visible on bare ground where mushrooms arise is mycelium. And the fruit of that involved union is what you seek.

(But more than edible mushrooms and comestible oddities belong to the fungus world. The mold that yields penicillin, yeasts used to brew beer and raise bread, even the organisms that flavor Roquefort cheese and cause athlete's foot are all bona fide members of this group.)

Acting as scavengers to digest dead or dying plant and animal life, the fungi of the woodlands continuously enrich the soil by breaking down decaying matter into humus. The entire chain of growth as we know it depends heavily on fungi. In a wet year it is impossible to walk down any path in late summer without literally stumbling over a profusion of interesting pop-ups. The fun of foraging consists precisely in reaping where you did not sow. Whoever can differentiate broccoli from cauliflower will be able to recognize at least the seven groups described here.

In Europe the commerce in mushrooms is vast, and the Swiss rank among the most avid seekers. My neighbor, who grew up in the canton of Valais, recounts that in his boyhood every village center had a mushroom expert on duty at the fire station on weekends. People would drift in with perplexing specimens for the resident mycologist to identify. Mushrooms were a staple of the diet; whole families went into the woods together in morel, or chanterelle, or bolete season.

It is possible to buy at least a dozen different kinds of wild fungi in the markets of Italy or Germany. In Russia and Poland wild fungi are a prime food. In America, until recently, suspicion and dread combined to keep even the common puffball off the market. Except for a few local farmers' markets, consumers were limited to the palatable but pale cultivated agaricus found in the supermarket. Now, however, it is possible to find three or four species, flown in from the Pacific Northwest, gracing the specialty vegetable section of big-city supermarkets.

Wild mushrooms take myriad forms. Some have gills, some have multiple pores, some have spines or teeth. Some resemble tropical corals, others take the shape of scallops or oysters. Still others are round or pear-shaped. One is even a direct mock-up of a dog's phallus. Commonly, the term *toadstool* was applied to whatever fungi were judged toxic or foul, in the folk belief that a toad had squatted on or under the offender and poisoned it. Today, the vegetable gardener has learned to cherish the toad for his ability to devour cutworms. And among mycophagists (mushroom eaters), toadstool is considered a cruel epithet to be disavowed along with various other racist and sexist expressions.

Not all mushrooms are safe to eat. Most of the mild troublemakers—those that can cause upset stomachs and vomiting—betray themselves by their disagreeable smell or extremely bitter or acrid taste. Some people are allergic to one or more species of wild fungi, just as they may be allergic to one or another vegetable or fruit. It is a good plan to eat only one new kind of mushroom at a time, and that in moderation.

It is an even better plan to know your enemy. Although other toxic varieties can cause severe illness, almost invariably the sixty to seventy mushroom fatalities occurring annually in the United States are due to the conspicuous, handsome amanita. Many members of this prolific clan are nonlethal, but nine of the amanitas are deadly poison. They contain phallotoxins and amatoxins, complex polypeptide molecules that liver enzymes convert into a compound that attacks liver cells. Slow to appear, this liver damage is irreversible. Reason enough to learn from the outset how to distinguish the amanitas and to give them a wide berth.

Attractive, showy, as seductive as the jacket of a trashy novel and displaying to the uninitiate all desirable mushroom qualities, the amanita nods its cap throughout the growing season. It can be found in deep or thin woods, along sun-dappled margins, and even, though rarely, in open fields.

Charles McIlvaine, writing in 1902 in his still unequaled tome, *One Thousand American Fungi* (reissued by Robert Mac-

Adam and Something Else Press, West Glover, Vermont, in 1973), has said of the amanitas: "They are the aristocrats of fungi. Their noble bearing, their beauty, their power for good or evil, and above all their perfect structure, have placed them first in their realm; and they proudly bear the three badges of their clan and rank—the volva or sheath from which they spring, the kid-like apron encircling their waists, and patch-marks of high birth upon their caps."

The volva or sheath of the amanita is not merely a bul-bous swelling at the foot of the stalk, but an in-ground bag-like cup out of which the stem arises. The apron, a remnant of the universal veil through which the button mushroom pushed upward into the light, tearing the veil as it expanded, stays on the stalk as a sort of tattered skirt or ring. As for the "patch-marks" McIlvaine speaks of, the novice hunter ought not to put too much credence in these often no-longer-visible warts. They can wash away in a prolonged rain.

All the poisonous amanitas have white or creamy-white gills. Until you are knowledgeable about gilled mushrooms in general, a wise rule is not to gather or to taste *any* white- or yellowish-white-gilled mushroom. This means bypassing some edible and delicious non-amanita varieties but the stakes are too high for an error.

Surely the safest place to begin your fungus foraging is with the non-gilled variety. A wise child makes an excellent accomplice, for instance, in stalking the agreeable, plain old puffball. A five-year-old stands comfortably close to the ground out of which the puffball emerges when it is not cropping up by the half-hundreds on rotting logs or tree stumps. At least a dozen different kinds lurk in the woods or spring forth on the edges of lawns or dot the manicured terrain of golf courses. They begin to show themselves in late spring, come into their own in midsummer, and run rampant into the fall. In our area of central New Hampshire, an afternoon's puffball haul can range from the tiny, talcum-powdered, pear-shaped lycoperdons to soccer-ball-sized crackled beige and brown calvatias. (On August 27, 1979, a *Calvatia gigantea* sighted from horseback and taken hostage in a woodland clearing was the size of a well-inflated beachball.) Any puffball with white innards is good to eat. Should you cut open the thick-skinned *Scleroderma,* its purply black inner flesh will repel your appetite, but even this bitter old bird is not dangerous.

No matter how minuscule it is, you must slice each puffball in half when preparing it for the table, just to be certain to differentiate it from a gilled mushroom in its infantile button stage. In this case the profile of a gilled mushroom will be clearly visible. Puffballs are white inside; they have the consistency of sponge cake or creamed farmer cheese. If the interior has begun to turn yellow or squashy, the specimen is too mature for the table. Puffballs need to be dealt with promptly after gathering, for, like garden corn, their shelf life is brief. You may encounter little battalions of them shriveled in the field after the crop has gone by. Clever children like to pick these and carry them about in secret, occasionally lifting one to their lips in the presence of a horrified adult, and squeezing out a puff of spores in imitation of cigarette smoke.

Practically nothing needs to be done to a puffball except to brush off any dirt or forest debris before slicing and frying in butter, margarine, or olive oil. The gigantic brownish ones, sometimes called brain puffballs, benefit from having the outer layer peeled before cooking. They can be dipped in beaten egg and breadcrumbs, like slices of eggplant; they can be tossed

into stews or soups. After sautéing, they can be frozen suc-
cessfully, but all too soon lose their rich flavor. Some people
slice and thread them and hang them up to dry. We like
them best fried crisp in slices, then salted and served with
cocktails. They are sure to provide your timorous guests with
lugubrious conversation for the balance of the evening.

The hedgehog or spine or teeth fungi are instantly iden-
tifiable by the presence of small downward-pointing spines on
the fruiting body in place of gills or pores. Some say they
look like tiny, evenly spaced icicles. The hedgehogs tend to
frequent areas of decaying wood, but may put in an appear-
ance in unlikely groves of live conifers and mixed hardwoods.
None is dangerous, although some may be too tough to warrant cooking.

Worth scouring the countryside for is the spreading
hedgehog mushroom, *Dentinum repandum,* or pig's trotter. At
first glance it looks not unlike an ordinary, though sunken,
mushroom from the top, often with its cap turning up around
the rim. But instead of gills on the undersurface, the pig's
trotter possesses characteristic little white teeth, almost like
rubber bristles. The stem is white or paler than the cap,
thick, usually crooked. The cap may range from pale tan to
a rusty yellow, but the flesh is white. These fungi most frequently occur in clusters and fruit from early summer into the
fall. Sturdy little guys up to four or five inches in diameter,
their reputation is irreproachable. Eat and enjoy. You will
swiftly learn to recognize the dramatic spiny teeth. A larger
variant with bigger teeth and a crackled to scaly cap is a *Hydnum.* Gather and deal with them in their freshest hour. They
are best stewed, so plan on longish cooking and add water or
broth as needed. A good crop will more than halve the amount
of beef you need to put in the pot; these fungi agreeably take

on the meat flavor and disguise themselves as chunks of bottom round.

The bear's head or Medusa-head and the *Hericium coralloides* are all large, fleshy masses in the shape, says one authority, of an ox's heart (I've never seen an ox's heart) that attach themselves to decaying wood. The discoverer need not distinguish one from another; all are edible. They are almost too beautiful to seize. A find is commonly the occasion for a party, since one specimen can weigh as much as twenty pounds. McIlvaine reports a relative, *Hydnum erinaceum* (now called *Hericium erinaceus*), on a dead beech tree in Eagle's Mere, Pennsylvania, weighing more than fifty pounds. (The author once came upon a fifteen-pound heist of bear's head gleaming from a rotted log; her husband gallantly gave up his shirt to fetch it home.) You may find only three or four of these giant white or dark cream excrescences in a lifetime of woods walking, so be prepared. Trim off the tough parts where the body was attached to its host and cook judiciously long enough to bring out the flavor. These do well in a fricassee or stew. The tender outer teeth, sautéed in butter until crisp, have a nutlike flavor.

The polypores are also tree-dwellers, and they are probably the most obvious fungi in the woods. Everyone has seen tough old "conks"—shelf-like protrusions adorning the torsos of aged trees—and most people have idly picked up dried birch polypores for the fun of drawing pictures on their flat white undersurfaces. While most polypores are far too tough—leathery or even woody—to eat, there are notable exceptions. The most common edible polypore in our region is *Polyporus sulphureus,* a layered yellow and orange effusion that goes by the popular name of chicken-of-the-woods. Clusters of sulfur polypore can be found from late spring into the fall. We rate it near the top of the list for flavor, texture, and versatility. I braise strips of sulfur polypore in butter, salt, and a little water, after which a quantity can be frozen for any upcoming casserole. Young specimens are best, at any season; old layers toughen as they dry out. In summer, insects invade the fruiting bodies, so it is wise to hunt for newly formed ones and to trim off the succulent, newer edges of old specimens. Polypores, as the name suggests, have multiple pores shaped like little tube mouths on their undersides in place of gills. Most species do not have any stem at all; if a stem is present, it is not centrally located, as in the bolete or in the ordinary supermarket agaricus, but grows laterally, offside as it were.

Polyporus squamosus, a dingy white-to-gray polypore whose top surface is larded with overlapping brown scales or squamules, pops out in spring on ancient tree stumps all along our woodland trails. Though safely edible, it is not a popular item with pickers, simply because it lacks flavor. (Some mushroom eaters will hotly dispute this statement.) I have had an immodest success slicing this plentiful fungus—old-timers sometimes call it dryad's saddle to describe the saddle shape it assumes as it grows—and hanging threaded strings of it to dry.

Fleshy types like these polypores will also dry politely on cookie sheets in an oven with a pilot light. Once all the pieces are bread-crumb dry, I strip them from the strings into a sterilized dry jar, sprinkle in a few peppercorns, and put the jars away for the winter. These provisions go far to filling out a spaghetti sauce, a soup, or a cold-weather stew. They reconstitute nicely in any liquid setting.

Polyporus frondosus, a rounder mass of many small overlapping caps, resembles, if you squint, a hen with her feathers fluffed out around a brood of chicks. Found near but not on rotted stumps, it is a prize. Alas, I have only encountered it once, but made it the occasion for a feast. Cut into manageable bite sizes, sautéed in butter, then braised in a little added liquid, this hen-of-the-woods has a crisp taste not unlike fresh filberts.

In our region, the corals, aptly named as they look exactly like the ocean variety, come up chiefly in pine groves, although they also occur under mixed hardwoods. Corals come in a variety of colors and sizes, ranging from pure white to yellow to amethyst. Slender ones, stubby ones, intricately branched tight clusters, and single-club "earth tongues" are easy for the novice to identify and safe to taste. Only one, the rare *Ramaria formosa* with orange-red branches and flesh that bruises black, is toxic. If any raw coral tastes bitter, discard it. To clean corals, soak them in cold salt water for a while; it is picky but companionable work dislodging the last little bits of pine needles, so I try to enlist a helper. Mild, white corals go nicely raw in a tossed salad. They pickle well, steeped in the same brew used for bread-and-butter cucumber pickles. Sautéed in butter over high heat, they turn to crisp nibbles and disappear during the cocktail hour.

A wild-looking, polypore-like mass, called sparassis, resembles an enormous misplaced head of curly lettuce attached to the base of a tree and is also classified as coral. The message is not to uproot, but to cut clear through your woods-lettuce a bit above ground level so it may regrow. Invite the neighbors in. Celebrate, sauté bits in butter, tumble into an ovenproof dish, dredge with bread crumbs and your favorite seasonings, bake slowly and enjoy. On August 30, less than a mile from home, we found a shy sparassis just off the trail. Since they tend to recur, I've memorized the spot and will revisit it in hopes of a second tryst.

No species are more rewarding to the causal fungus gatherer than the boletes. From the top or in profile they are often mistaken by beginners for true gilled mushrooms. But the underside of the bolete consists of tube mouths through which the spores are discharged. The spongy underside may be thick or thin and range in color from red to yellow to white. The stalk of the bolete is quite fleshy and may be scaly or smooth, solid-colored or striped. There are so many boletes—many more than there are kinds of corals, for instance—that the casual collector is frequently foiled in his efforts to distinguish among them. Unless a bolete has red tube mouths or turns a vivid blue when broken open, it is entirely safe to try raw. August 9, in the woods, our trail was literally crowded with young fresh specimens of a bolete I cannot name. Its tube mouths were white to buff-colored, the top wine-red and dry. The flesh, pure white, tasted delicious raw. Once they had been adjudged choice, we took all we could stuff into our packs. Most now repose, sautéed, in the freezer. The rest enlivened a hamburger gravy.

Insect infestation poses the chief problem with these varied and safe species. You need almost to be in the vicinity as the bolete crowds its way up from the forest floor, at least early in the season. Larvae make any mushroom bitter, but they seem to invade boletes first of all. Later, when the nights are cooler and insects lethargic, the boletes stay firm even in their mature state. If the tube mouths are squashy, you can discard them. If the tops are slimy, they can be peeled.

The French call their best bolete, *Boletus edulis,* the *cèpe.* The Germans say *Steinpilz.* In Europe, they can be found in cans at the supermarket.

Other kinds of boletes, ranging from one that resembles a pine cone (*Strobilomyces floccopus*) to one with mottled red hairs rather suggesting a Victorian hall wallpaper (*Suillus pictus*) are worth experimenting with. A *Boletinellus,* with a dry, dark brown top, radiating yellow-veined undersurface, and an off-center, primitive stem, runs rampant under our ash trees and is routinely ground up by the lawnmower. Today I read in Phyllis Glick's wonderful handbook* that this fellow is edible but "needs special treatment. Marinate in highly seasoned wine or lemon-oil dressing, dip in beaten egg, roll in bread crumbs, fry." I probably won't, on grounds that even cardboard treated this royally would be rendered edible, but it cheers me to think that someone cares enough to deal so lovingly with this humble and ubiquitous critter.

Ah, the chanterelle! We prize it above all other species. Normally, our chanterelle season runs for about four weeks, beginning early in July (once, on June 26). The little yellow vases can be found unfailingly in the same place year after year. We always try to extend our range, since chanterelles rarely occur in great clusters, preferring to tease the quester ever onward into deeper and deeper woods. The most common of our local chanterelles, the *cibarius,* is chrome yellow, dry, and seldom stands as tall as three inches. The outer surface has blunt-edged veins running down the stem, lacing themselves into an intricate pattern. If you happen on a much larger, bright orange clump with knife-sharp, regular gills, you have found the false chanterelle, a jack-o'-lantern mushroom that used to be called *Clitocybe illudens* and is now properly *Omphalotus olearius.* (Mushroom nomenclature is in a constant state of evolution.) It is reputed to glow in the dark—clearly enough so that the viewer can distinguish the gills!—and is toxic. But it resembles a chanterelle about as much as cauli-

---

*Phyllis Glick, *The Mushroom Trail Guide.* (New York: Holt, Rinehart & Winston, 1979).

flower resembles broccoli, so fear not. *Cantharellus umbonatus* is a grayish-white chanterelle with a little knob (umbo) in the center of the cap. You'll know it by its habitat, for it always grows in moss, and you can never pick one without getting a little blob of moss at the base along with the mushroom.

Another edible chanterelle presents itself from time to time in our woods. The horn of plenty (otherwise known as the trumpet of death) is grayish brown to black on the outside, hollow in the center, and has a smooth or only slightly rumpled sort of exterior surface. Luckily, when these little funeral directors arrive, they arrive in a grand army, enough to make a meal. They are a taste treat fried in butter or, for the cholesterol-conscious, a light olive oil. Last year we found in gratifying numbers a new-to-us chanterelle, *Craterellus canthar-ellus,* little ruffled numbers ranging from pale pink to salmon with yellow stems. They were still fruiting on September 1.

Last of all, because it is mildly tricky to differentiate, let us consider the morel. First comer in the season, up in May in New Hampshire, early April in Virginia, the morel is considered by epicures the world around to be the finest of the fungi. This convoluted, spongelike, honeycomb-tripe-pitted delicacy grows two to four inches high, in shades of dingy brown or gray, with a lighter stem. Its habitat is mysterious. Hunters will tell you to check out apple orchards, follow elm tree roots, wander on burned-over ground, but the true morel seeker will keep his sources secret. A friend from western Pennsylvania writes: "The entire countryside goes berserk in season, people avoid each other and sneak into alien fields, one woman was killed by a truck last summer while searching! I read somewhere morels are now selling for two hundred fifty dollars a pound! Is this possible?"

Treasure your morels. Rinse clean in cold water, slice

down the middle—the true morel will be hollow all the way through—dry on towels of cloth or paper. You can bake, sauté, dry, or freeze (cooked or uncooked) your versatile storehouse of bites. Don't overseason; let the true flavor prevail.

Now the caveat. While in Europe and in the Pacific Northwest people gather, eat, and thrive on various false morels—*Gyromitra, Helvella, Verpa*—evidence now suggests these are toxic and should be avoided. The so-called false morels are easily distinguishable from the true-blue ones; their caps are attached to the top of the stem, or to only the upper portion of the stem, and hang about it like a little skirt. Once you slice through a true morel, you will instantly see the difference. Moreover, false morels are not actually pitted, but merely wrinkled or deeply folded. Morels have honeycomb pits all over their caps. A case of broccoli versus cauliflower once more!

Best of all, go moreling the first season with an old-timer and learn your craft in situ. And by all means, begin to amass your own five-foot shelf of mushroom books. My current favorite is the aforementioned Glick handbook, but the fungus bibliography is continually enlarging and endlessly fascinating. See you in the chanterelle patch!

Bringing Up
Boomerang

Some of my writer friends traveled in Europe last summer. One holed up in Nantucket and completed a draft of a novel. Several served on the staffs of writers' conferences. I spent three months in rural New Hampshire ministering to an orphan foal.

How does a human get so involved with horses that she can spend hours every day in their large and redolent company?

It goes like this. When I was a small child growing up in Philadelphia's then-fashionable suburb of Germantown, the garbage wagons were still drawn by horses. So were most of the milk wagons. One winter I gave away my three older brothers' camp blankets to various forlorn-looking draft horses as they toiled up our hill.

It wasn't as if there had been no animals in my life; on the contrary, we were a family that "had" dogs. A succession of them ran away or were struck by cars or were poisoned by phobic neighbors. It seemed we were always beginning again with a puppy, which was never allowed abovestairs and each night was incarcerated in the cavernous cellar. When the poor beast howled at night, I frequently snuck down into the gloom and curled up with it on the discarded shag rug allotted for its bed. The cellar was warm and the rug was a thick one, but my deed was more heroic than it sounds. I was terrified of the dark, but even more terrified that turning on a light would alert my parents. In those days, sensible children reserved their most extreme fear for the wrath of the elders.

Cats were forbidden; my mother never trusted cats. They were known to leap into baby carriages and suck away the infant's breath. I confess I never developed anything deeper than respect for cats. They are good mousers who keep the barn free of vermin.

Horses, surprisingly, *were* considered respectable creatures. I was permitted to take weekly riding lessons at a nearby livery stable, but punished for staying late to groom and feed and shovel manure. In truth, as the youngest of four children I felt an empathy with the animal world that was not manifest in the human one. I was wanted. I was doing a job. Moreover, manure mixed with wood shavings smelled better to me than perfume. At the risk of acquiring a reputation for coprophilia, I confess it still does.

Shall we now take into account Sigmund Freud and the Horse as Phallus? The young girl's interest in horses, according to the Master, is the socially acceptable sublimation of her sex drive. Horses symbolize dominance. Girls love the feeling of being in control of, and astride, all that power. When boys come cantering into the normal girl's life, horses back out of it. By implication, those females who experience no diminution of interest in horses after the onset of puberty are locked in internal struggle, ripe for neuroses, and will in time provide a rich pasture for the expensive romp of the psychoanalyst.

I deny nothing. I attend all hypotheses *qua* hypotheses. Freud's theories of female sexuality have now been substantially discredited, if not debunked. But the pathology of my own case is clearly linked to those dark-green, all-wool camp blankets with their embroidered S for Camp Shoshonee that rode down Carpenter Lane one by one on the bony rumps of the garbage collectors' jades. All my childhood I was a closet "Keeper of the Beasts." It seems I am still collecting and blanketing—rugging, it's called—the castoffs.

The story of Boomerang, my orphan foal, begins with such a rescue mission. Two years ago, for the price she was to fetch from the slaughterer, I bought a sad-eyed, gravely undernourished mare. Taboo was a topography of saddle sores. Her tongue had been torn nearly in two with a wire bit. Her vertebrae and hipbones were vividly enough defined to provide an anatomy lesson for a zoology class. Her owner, operating on the theory that the less you feed a spirited horse the slower it will go, had been starving her, to no avail; she had run off with her last three riders.

Taboo was gradually restored to normal horse silhouette. I exercised her on the longe* line at first; the horse describes a circle around the trainer and learns to walk, trot, and canter on voice command. Then I rode her, timorously, while a friend worked the longe line. Finally, unattached, I began to walk and trot her in the ring. She was wonderfully smooth and responsive.

That spring, when I went trail-riding for the first time with a friend, Taboo clamped down on the bit and ran away with me for two miles. We raced her mythological wolves at a flat-out gallop down a hard-packed dirt road at high noon. The wind rushed in my mouth and took away my breath.

*French for long. Sometimes spelled as it is pronounced, *lunge*, the movement has nothing to do with a sudden thrust or plunge.

Dying will be like this, I thought. Dying will happen around the next bend. Luckily, I met no one coming the other way, although I remember glimpsing a very surprised fisherman as we clattered over a wooden bridge and flew inexorably onward.

Having survived that forty-mile-an-hour ordeal, I learned to ride out alone, and to canter only on the steepest hills so I could somewhat control this schizophrenic mare.

Why don't you breed her? my horse friends all suggested as the season turned. Mares have a way of settling down after they're bred. You'll see how calm and docile she'll be after she's had a foal.

Taboo came unmistakably and definitively into heat on June 30. She squealed and squirted urine and rubbed her tail on the barn side until the top hairs fell out. Awaj, the local Arabian stallion, serviced her on each of four successive mornings. Forty-nine days later, she caught me in an inattentive moment and ran away with me again. Once I had her in hand, I walked home, shaken. It was no use. She would have to go to the knacker. Death and dog food awaited this beautiful crazy horse. Then, just like in a television soap, the vet called with news of the blood test. Taboo had "settled"; Awaj had gotten her pregnant.

And she did settle down as the pregnancy progressed. During the last two months of that eleven-month-long gestation, I rode her bareback so as to spare her the discomfort of the girth around her swollen barrel. It was blackfly time; I wore a beekeeper's hat to defend against them. She wore her gauze ear-bonnet, which ties under the throat, for the same purpose. Since she was shoeless, I put on the winter Easyboots, weird but effective contraptions of polyurethane that are custom-designed for each hoof. Even so, they have a way of coming loose in snow, and since they are notoriously hard to locate, white on white, I had painted them red. Thus sallied forth the eccentric woman and her strangely gotten-up horse with its red toenails!

On the night of June 2, Taboo foaled. The little buckskin filly was on her feet whinnying in a moment. And then the nightmare began. The mare, snorting with panic in a far corner of the stall, would not allow the newborn to approach her. Each time it nosed blindly against her flanks, hungry to suck, she bit and kicked it.

A frantic call to the vet at one a.m. Never had I felt guiltier, not even when I awakened the pediatrician for advice about earache. Twitch the mare and back her into a corner every two hours, was the vet's advice. If the foal doesn't get the colostrum—the first milk secreted by the mammary glands immediately after birth—it won't get the antibodies necessary for its survival. A twitch, for the uninitiate, is a metal pincers or loop of rope used to restrain a horse by tightening it around the animal's upper lip. Even subdued with a twitch and with her hindquarters backed into a corner of the stall where she could do the least damage kicking, Taboo was a terror. The pathetic little battered foal went on fighting for her birthright, getting ten or twelve hungry sucks at a time.

We went through this medieval torture every two hours around the clock for the first day, every four hours thereafter. On the morning of the third day we separated the two forever. Taboo the unwilling mother, turned out to pasture, recovered rapidly. Boomerang the foal, imprinted from the first on the intervening humans who had saved her life, regards people still as her mother-surrogates. We bottle-fed her for about four days and then were able to wean her to a pail. This is easier than it sounds; horses drink by sucking rather than lapping. The amazing thing was how rapidly thirty-two ounces of formula went down. Because Boomerang's forelegs were too long

and her neck too short to drink from a pail set on the ground—
after all, nature had designed her to suckle standing up—we
built a little stand on pegs to hold the bowl of milk. A few
weeks later, we did the same with a grain box.

It was hard not to hate the rejecting mare. It was even
harder to put up with the jocularity about women's lib that
she and I were subject to. For half the town turned out to
ogle at the miracle of the orphan foal who had not only survived her ordeal but showed every sign of growing up to be a
well-made pedigreed filly. I developed a certain paranoia. How
many minutes into the conversation would it take for each
man who sauntered up the hill to say something terribly clever
and snide about the role of the female?

Nodding his head at the mare grazing in an adjoining
pasture, my farrier said, "Guess she's been readin' *Ms.* magazine" (one minute).

The vet, an affable, unflappable man, bending over to
stitch the foal's worst cut, offered, "You shouldn't've given
her all those books on bein' modern" (two minutes, thirty
seconds).

"That's a damn smart mare," the man who raises vealers
said. "Why'n't you get her some trousers and she can go to
the city?" (twenty seconds).

I remembered the look of terror in the mare's eyes, how
she quivered and trembled when the foal struggled out of the
amniotic sac, rocked and swayed finding its balance, and stag-
gered toward her. She seemed to say, "What happened? I
had a little cramp and lay down for a minute and when I got
up there was a ghost in the stall!"

I remembered my own terror in childbirth-before-the-
Enlightenment: how alien that screaming bundle of raw flesh
seemed, wrapped in white cloth and presented to my awkward
arms!

I remembered how excruciating the nursing process had been. My nipples cracked and bled afresh with every session. After five days of agony every four hours, I capitulated. The hungry baby made a happy transition to bottled formula. I came down with what was then called "milk fever" and suffered the conclusion that I was not made for suckling my young. That deprived infant and the two who followed were raised on cow's milk and Karo syrup diluted with water and boiled to a fare-thee-well.

And I remembered the hiss of discomfort, that sharp intake of breath on the mare's part every time the foal nuzzled its way to her milk bag. When the little one finally clamped onto a teat, the mare was almost unrestrainable. Pain, I thought, unmitigated by maternal instinct or social pressure. Sigmund, where are you now when I need you? I was relating all over the place.

It is not unflattering to be followed about by a foal. The general public does not realize that you represent *milk*. The general public cherishes a fantasy of loyalty, love, and little-lamb enduring values. That filly would have left me in an instant for a welcoming mare with milk in her bag. As it was, she had to make do with Borden's Foal-Lac, a milk replacer supplemented with every known vitamin and trace mineral and almost as expensive, ounce for ounce, as good Scotch whisky. The twenty-five-pound cans (at thirty-three dollars a can) come impishly illustrated with a photograph of a cow wearing a saddle and bridle, an anomaly I came to loathe at two in the morning as I mashed and stirred the lumpy formula into a potable gruel. Since our other horses are turned out all night in summer, at least I did not have to contend with a barnful of inquisitive equines when I went down with the copper bowl from an old chafing dish which exactly fitted the stand we had built.

May it be said in Borden's favor that they also manufacture Foal-Lac in pellet form. By the end of the first month, Boomer had acquired four teeth and a certain hazy notion of the texture of solids. She spilled as many as she chewed, but came to love a mixture of regular grain and the magic expensive pellets. We kept her on her early morning "fix" of warm formula, however, long after the other milk feedings had been gradually and sneakily withdrawn. The first morning I arrived in her stall with pellets and grain only, she knocked me flat in her ten-week-old zeal to discover where the hot milk was hiding.

Even so, in a way it was less traumatic than the normal weaning. All too often, mare and foal shriek piteously to each other for days after separation. And then, just when your sanity has eroded to the hardpan madness that lurks beneath all our frontal lobes, they lose interest in each other.* Six weeks after that, they have forgotten the maternal-filial relationship altogether. They are, miraculously, strangers and may now become friends. . . . Not without its appeal, that notion, to us mothers for life.

What a mare teaches her foal are the normal precautionary measures even a domestic beast must take: flee the unusual sound or movement; be wary of strangers; come when called, and above all, emulate me. On the first day of Boomer's life a septic tank was being installed, an operation that involved a backhoe and a bulldozer not fifty feet from her stall. Carpentry, meanwhile, was proceeding overhead to the tune of an air compressor that seats the started nails and stutters like a machine gun. With that for normal background noise, there is little indeed that spooks this filly. As for caution regarding

---

*Experience has since taught the author that weaning is far easier if the mare is removed from the foal, after the first month, for gradually increasing periods each day.

strangers, people in her orphan brain are safe and warm and food-providing. Thus she has accepted the halter and lead shank almost without question. She stands to have her feet lifted one by one and tapped on in preparation for the age when she will be shod. Come when called, yes, and answer with a whinny. She greets me at feeding time with a basso little nicker. As for emulation, the situation is fuzzy. Instinct has prevailed; she has learned to graze. She bucks and rears and races for the hell of it, dodging about as nimbly as a goat, and when she runs at her happiest, she carries her tail straight up, like a deer's scut.

Today, Boomerang is five months old and growing fast. The trees are leafless now. There is a cutting edge to the north wind. Nature has responded by providing her with a fuzzy winter coat, far thicker than the coats adult horses develop each autumn. I've just spent an hour repairing a stretch of fence that had yielded to some large-scale leanings and scratchings. As I head back down the pasture toward the barn, Boomer whinnies shrilly. She is torn between staying in the field with the other horses and following me to the paddock. I don't turn back. She hesitates, then, just before I drop out of her line of vision, comes racing after me. I stay for a few minutes in the paddock, tousling her much as you might tousle a large dog. She nuzzles and nudges me for more. As with an affectionate dog, more is never enough. After I duck through the fence and head toward the house, she stands for a few minutes at the rail to make sure I mean it. Finally, she trots back out to the upper field, rejoining the herd.

She has taken up a lot of slack in my life, that one. Between teaching commitments and my own writing, to say nothing of the daily exigencies of a country life in which we grow our own vegetables and cut our own wood, it is a life not noted for slack to begin with. But living in and with the world of the physical is a release from the world of the mind. Paradoxically, I find mucking out stalls each morning a fine and private time for thinking. The poet in me is fed. I am deeply nurtured, I think, by the animals I deal with and observe, from the chipmunk that lurks under Boomer's feedbox or the fox that enters the paddock at night to sit and bark, to the horses themselves, those immense presences. "Animals are honest through their inability to lie," I said in a poem. Their instinctual responses, their lack of guile, their physical grace, and their intellectual limitations all move and work in me.

And of all animals, surely a foal is the chief aesthetic delight. Sometimes, leaving Taboo out of it, I think how much I'd like another one. Anybody out there with a proven broodmare in need of a kind home?

Epilogue: Boomer grew up to be a creditable competitive trail horse. She has earned her thousand-mile award and is well on the way to her two-thousand. Much as we would like to pass on her stamina and grit, we haven't had the courage to breed her, fearful that she too may lack the requisite maternal instinct to suckle a foal. She has never lost that ear-splitting, peremptory whinny that summons humans to the fence gate at feeding time or announces the uphill arrival of the horse trailer with some other equine aboard. Now the alpha-mare of the group, she keeps order mercilessly among the shifting population of youngsters. All hay piles are hers until she chooses one. No one may enter the barn until her stall door has been opened. But she is safe and sane under saddle, fearless among dogs or in traffic. Our prodigal, she will be with us always.

The Family Saddle Horse

I have a recurring dream. In it the stalls of the Family Horses are mucked out by a magical robot wielding a ten-tine fork and trundling a hefty wheelbarrow. Fresh sawdust, shavings, or straw bedding is then evenly distributed, water buckets are scrubbed out and refilled, the happy robot humming all the while. The horses themselves are fed and groomed, any visible scratches or bites are dressed, and they are then led off in the proper order—bossy gelding first, then the mare, then the filly—to the upper pasture. Although it is winter, in my dream they graze, untroubled by deerflies, on timothy and clover.

The robot then busies itself cleaning bridles and saddles, doing an honest job, taking the equipment apart into its nasty little component straps and buckles rather than swiping halfheartedly at the exposed places. The robot reassembles the tack skillfully, never once having to slip the headstall of a bridle onto its own cranium in order to get the bit and reins going in the right directions.

This versatile robot drives a truck as well. It goes cheerfully across town for grain, hay, hoof dressing, salt blocks, and special vitamins for the pregnant mare. After that, it repairs to the sawmill for a load of fresh shavings, which it shovels tirelessly into the bin in the barn. All that remains for me and other members of the family is to ride the Family Horses.

In truth, Family Horses are by definition tended to by the family. Even meeting the minimum daily requirements of horse care is time-consuming and certainly less onerous if chores are shared. But goodwill is not enough. I would like to assume that no one acquires a Family Horse without first acquiring the basic necessary skills and knowledge for its care.

It's cruel not to know, for example, that a horse permitted to blunder into the grain supply will eat itself to death by way of a painful illness called founder. Or that to offer grain or water to a panting, sweating horse fresh from the trail is to invite at the very least an attack of colic. Taking on a pet horse is considerably more complicated than adding a cat or dog to the hearth.

In its most relaxed version the Family Horse shapes up as a pony borrowed or rented for the summer to graze peaceably in a well-fenced field furnished with a three-sided shelter popularly known as a loafing shed. The field is so fertile and the animal such an easy keeper that it requires only a coffee can of grain or pelleted feed morning and night. The child so loves the pony that it receives daily grooming from its small person-owner. The pony is ridden every day, weather permitting. Once the autumn chill is on the land and the grass stops growing, this family returns to its other life in the city. The pony and the wethered goat that kept it company go back to their starting point to await another June.

But more and more adults are coming down with the highly contagious horse fever. One small New Hampshire town of fifteen hundred souls supports three riding schools, two with indoor arenas for year-round lessons. Hardly a weekend passes without a pleasure or competitive trail ride, gymkhana, three-phase event, or backyard horse show on the calendar.

Assorted colors, breeds, and temperaments can be seen in action at these events. A cat may look at a king and a Shetland pony at a Thoroughbred. Probably most Family Horses are grade animals, horses without pedigrees. Some school horses are available at the end of summer for as little as $250. The registered Arabian or Thoroughbred, the purebred quarter horse or Appaloosa, can run to ten or more times that sum.

When shopping for a horse, the prospective owner always asks the seller to ride the beast under scrutiny to demonstrate its skills. Before concluding the bargain the new owner-to-be always cheerfully pays the veterinarian's fee to have the Family Dobbin-to-be checked for soundness, putative age, and general good health.

Ideally, Family Horses are physically fit enough to carry the parents on twenty-five-mile competitive trail rides; they are interchangeable mounts the kids can ride as well. Reasonably schooled for equitation or pleasure classes, Family Horses load sensibly, after a little coaxing, into the family or rented trailer. Above all, they hack safely in traffic, go well in the company of strange horses, and only race at the gallop when invited to do so.

Family Horses recognize their owners, nickering when they catch sight of a member of the family. More often than not they come when called, especially once the bloom is off the clover in the pasture. They enjoy attention and stand quietly while being tended. They eat apple, carrot, summer squash, and corncob tidbits from the family's hands, once these treats have been broken in horse-size bites for safe swallowing. Ingratiating, honest horses, they neither kick nor bite nor rear,

[37]

although a mild buck or two under saddle is acceptable when the weather turns brisk in the fall or when the grass greens up in the spring.

In theory, then, the Family Horse is the perfect horse. It is reliable but not stodgy, energetic but not hard-mouthed. Spirited, yet obedient. Calm, yet interested. It does not step on the children's toes and it is friends with the family dog.

In actuality, Family Horses change with the changing expectations of the family riders. What they have in common is that they are loved. Each has some personality trait that endears it to its owners.

Our first Family Horse was an overweight palomino gelding the color and consistency of a pound of butter at room temperature. Elephant Child loved to be groomed. He was willing to stand all day in crossties if someone would curry or brush him or comb out his luxuriant mane and tail. His disposition was so placid that he seldom glanced sideways when motorcycles roared past. Raging dogs barely caused him to quicken his pace. He was the only horse I ever knew that could eat along the trail at a trot. Wherever anything edible loomed, Elephant Child sidled, snatching, alongside.

Elephant Child wasn't good for much. As we improved, he seemed less desirable. He couldn't keep up with other horses on the trail, he showed no talent for jumping the smallest obstacles, he never cantered more than ten strides unless flogged, and none of us had an appetite for flogging. We faced the fact. What we had was the perfect Beginner's Horse. Elephant Child moved on to another family in our town where he is performing the same function that he so patiently served for us.

Since that time we have always kept a minimum of two Family Horses, for equines are gregarious creatures and horseback riding is a companionable sport. Any animal that doesn't come in the house at night deserves a companion, runs my private credo, though perfectly well adjusted single horses do exist.

Our horses are bedded in stalls at ground level in an old hillside barn once designed for cattle. Although in clement weather the horse may need only a loafing shed or a stand of pine trees for shade in the heat of the day, winter is a sterner story. A dry shelter out of the wind is absolutely essential. Indeed, New Hampshire law requires every owner of livestock to provide at least a three-sided structure for his beasts. A reasonable punishment for scofflaws in my opinion would be a February night in the open. The Family Horse owner sleeps justly when the wind whips across the ridge and rattles the panes of the house knowing that the Family Horses are stabled on dry bedding out of the cutting blast.

Obviously, the horse in winter needs more calories to keep warm. The beast that stayed sassy fat from May until September on pastureland with very little supplemental feed may now require five or six sections, or flakes, of hay a day to maintain its shape. Weight loss shows up most prominently along the top line of the horse, where hip- and backbones may suddenly become visible. Alarming hollows may appear in a once-rounded neck. The Family Horse owner is not deceived by the shapeliness of the beast's underbelly, which may remain portly while ribs show razor-sharp.

But how much hay, and what kind? How much grain or pelleted feed? The answer is evasive because horses' needs vary widely. One animal may be such an easy keeper that three sections of hay and four quarts of complete feed maintain its handsome figure. Another, highly strung or merely playful, may require two or three times those amounts to keep it horsing around. A good idea is to check with the former owner and to reproduce initially not only the amounts being fed but preferably also the very brand of feed. When switching types of feed, it's best to make the transition gradually.

The horse's stomach is a very little box compared with the animal's overall immensity, and holds only three or four gallons at a time. Nature must have dozed off while evolving the equine; it cannot vomit or even belch. Everything it ingests travels more than a hundred feet before it is expelled. The horse is a browser, designed for continuous nibbling. In its wild state it may graze as many as twenty hours out of every twenty-four. In captivity, so to speak, it will appreciate hay that is free of dust or mold, sweet to smell, and low in weed or bramble content. We feed hay that contains timothy and clover as well as native grasses, but with little or no alfalfa in it. Timothy is the standard hay of New England; it grows well in our climate, and when properly dried, stores well too. Alfalfa is the richest, sweetest, and most nutritious of the hays, but it is too rich for many equine digestive tracts and can be quite laxative. Today's processed feeds are so scientifically planned to feed the Whole Horse* that hay serves more as roughage and bulk than as protein in the average Family Horse's diet. And be it Agway or Blue Seal, Purina or other, virtually every feed sack carries a label of suggested weights and measurements for the daily feeding of the pleasure and show horse, the lactating mare, the weanling foal, and so on. The Family Horse owner can immerse himself in feed tables and texts.

---

*For example, the following ingredients are listed on the label of a feed sack containing horse ration pellets guaranteed to provide fourteen percent crude protein: ground oats, ground yellow corn, rice mill feed/oat hulls, dehydrated alfalfa meal (ethoxyquin added as a preservative), solvent-extracted linseed meal, cane molasses, wheat bran, wheat middlings, dehulled solvent-extracted soybean meal, hominy feed, salt, calcium carbonate, monocalcium phosphate, dicalcium phosphate, potassium sulphate, magnesium oxide, manganese oxide, cobalt carbonate, calcium iodate, zinc oxide, ferrous sulphate, riboflavin, calcium pantothenate, niacin, choline chloride, vitamin A (with improved stability), D-activated animal sterol, vitamin E.

Horse books abound, sage with advice and admonition, and occasional contradiction. Soon the Family Horse owner will be forced to add another shelf to his library, for new tomes on equine behavior keep turning up as birthday and anniversary presents, crowding out the special cookbooks.

We don't blanket our horses except in cases of illness. They grow shaggy protective coats and stay hardy. But on the bitterest days of winter I lavish the hay around, frequently tossing out an extra half-bale at midday when the mercury hangs sullenly at six below and the wind-chill factor equals thirty degrees below zero. There is no such thing as too much hay in bleak weather, except for the animal being kept in top condition for show ring or race course. The occasional poor beast who is allergic to hay may thrive on sun-dried alfalfa cubes instead. A block of combined minerals and salt in each stall gives the horse something nutritionally essential to lick or nibble at will. But unless a horse is getting regular work, it probably ought not be allowed to splurge on grain. Our big gelding, normally a model of decorum, turns into a bucking bronco in winter if he is overfed.

Paradise for a winter horse-owner is a frost-free water supply in the barn. Hauling water buckets by the sloshing pailful is downright painful in the hard season, but it can be done. Potable water at all times is an absolute must. A horse can survive longer unfed than it can unwatered. And what to do about icing up? After one winter of breaking through the top layer of ice in the tub with a pickaxe each morning, we invested in a little electric gadget that keeps the water temperature at about fifty degrees. At night the tub can be covered with boards or canvas to retain some of that precious heat. Admittedly, water buckets in the stalls still glaze over during the night, but this is Destiny in New England, and must be borne.

[41]

Good food, fresh water, decent shelter all go for naught if the horse is not protected against disease. All equines need annual injections in the spring to guard them from dreaded encephalitis and tetanus infections. These should be performed by the Family Vet, whose role is not dissimilar from that of the Family Pediatrician. Like the pediatrician, the vet frequently has "calling hours," a set time of day when he or she can be reached by phone for advice on a variety of complaints. Our veterinarian is a patient, remarkably equable man who can and frequently does work miracles.

Horses also need to be wormed at regular intervals, a procedure the owner can undertake on the advice of the vet. In the old days, an intelligent, finicky horse could smell the worm medicine mixed into its feed no matter how heavily the potion was laced with molasses, applesauce, peanut butter, or granola. But now, a dull-tipped, preloaded syringe makes dosing easy. The tip is inserted in a corner of the beast's mouth. The flavored medication gets squirted onto the animal's tongue and goes down the gullet without fuss. All praise to modern technology!

Not to worm faithfully is to invite disaster. A parasite-infested horse is a sad, lackluster creature. No matter how much it eats, its ribs are always sharply visible. It has no energy; nothing is any fun. And no wonder. It is being consumed alive inside. Moreover, there is no repairing severe parasite damage once stomach or intestinal walls have been weakened by attrition.

"No hoof, no horse!" reads the admonition blazoned on my farrier's van. While the horse that is ridden only on the yielding tanbark of an indoor arena can get by without shoes, the widely ranging Family Horse that hacks across town traveling sometimes on tar, frequently on rocky trails, and most often on hard-packed dirt roads needs regular attention. The farrier will trim hoofs, advise what kind and weight of shoe is best, and correctively shoe to help overcome certain common problems. One horse may require toe clips to keep its friable front hoofs from cracking. Another may need raised calks on the hind shoes to correct the animal's stride, so that the toes of the hind feet do not catch on or forge against the heels of the front feet.

A good many horses ridden on competitive trail rides are shod with heavy-duty pads on the front hoofs to protect the frog, the tender portion of the hoof, from stone bruises. Usually in winter all shoes are pulled and the horses go barefoot, which allows the hoof to toughen as it grows. For hard-core winter horseback riders, a polyurethane boot has been developed to provide excellent traction on snow. The boot, worn only while on the trail, can further be outfitted with borium-tipped studs, much like snow tire studs, for additional grip on ice. Although the initial outlay is about twenty dollars per foot, we have found the Easyboot a very workable arrangement. Ours are entering their third season of hard use, and except for the worn-down studs, replaceable each winter, they show no signs of wearing out.

What does the Family Horse, comfortably shod, sensibly wormed, housed and fed, wear on its head and back? Properly fitted equipment, of course. Bridles and saddles need not be new to be serviceable. Old leather, unless it is badly cracked, responds gratefully to cleaning and oiling. Many a useful bridle has been assembled from odds and ends of cheekpieces and headstalls, nosebands and reins, drawn from earlier eras and other horses' lives. Many an ancient saddle has been handed down from Grandpa's cavalry days.

But the Family Horse owner takes care that the tack fits

the horse. For example, an animal with prominent withers—thought to be a mark of nobility—will suffer bruising and sores if a saddle with a spread tree presses down on its bony protuberance. A round-barreled beast with no visible withers to snug the saddle in place may need a breastplate to keep the rig squarely on its back. It goes without saying that the saddle pad, covering the entire area, is to saddle as butter to bread.

As for bridling, such unintentional cruelties as a bit that hangs too low in the mouth, a bit that is too short and pinches the corners of the mouth, or too severe a bit for a soft-mouthed animal are responsible for many of the sour or skittish or undependable mounts every horse person encounters at some time. Most tack shops sell outgrown or no-longer-useful items that range from child-size stirrups to running martingales, as well as used saddles and bridles, at a fraction of their original cost.

The rewards for the Family Horse owner's labors are not entirely visible. Certain ones lodge in the cockles of the heart. When, on a fierce, blizzardy morning, the owner reluctantly puts feet to floor, jacket to frame, dons boots and gloves, and sallies forth to the barn, a chorus of nickers arises from the throats of the Family Horses. The basso profundo of the bossy gelding mingles with the middle voice of the mare. The ecstatic greetings of the yearling filly, sounding in the upper register, override them both.

Hunger does this, the Family Horse owner thinks, measuring out the morning feeding, undeceived by their earnest song. Hunger, and one thing more. Call it trust.

Building Fence

Making fences presupposes not only pastures but a storehouse of diligence. When you start from a tangle of sumac and blackberry, every reclaimed square yard seems more precious than an acre of riverbottom land. For a dozen years we've been pushing back the forest, clearing, seeding, and sustaining what now adds up to fourteen up-and-down acres of the once two hundred-odd that nurtured a dairy herd between the two world wars.

Building the fence itself is an imperfect science. Despite actual measurements, you have to yield to the contours of the land. Post holes are soul destroyers. Technology hasn't done much for the fence line on a hill farm. Even if you hire a neighbor's tractor with auger attachment, at least half the holes will have to be hand crafted as you ease them this side or that of expectation. Stones annoy, rocks impede, boulders break your heart as you tunnel down at a slant, hunting in vain for the earth bottom. If obdurate ledge or obstinate pudding stone does not require acts of faith and leaps of imagination, here and there you can count on a slope too steep for machinery to navigate. The gasoline-powered two-man auger is more adaptable, but even that ingenious tool will not maneuver between stump and bedrock with the same agility as the old manual clamshell tool.

Setting the posts exacts more faith from the dogged fence-pilgrim. Somehow there is never enough dirt in the pile you took out, even after you've placed a ring of stones in the bottom of the hole to brace the post. Even with a ring of stones stomped in nearly at the top for further support, your supply of loose dirt has vanished. You end up digging part of a second hole to make enough friable earth to hold the first pole solid. Clearly, you do not come out even.

You've set 225 posts, roughly ten feet apart. From an appropriate distance, if you squint, it's merely a toothpick stockade, inconclusive and raw-looking. You long to get on with it, to establish the feeling of fence, the ethos of enclosure.

The best part of building the fence is tacking up the string that denotes where the line of top boards means to be. You go around importantly to do this light work, trailing your ball of twine, wearing your apron of nails. You measure with your fold-up rule fifty-two inches from the ground—but where exactly *is* the ground? This mound, this declivity, this solitary flat patch? You tap in a nail, pull the string taut from the previous post, catch it with a few easy twists around, and so on. String stands in for wood, a notion, a suggestion of what's to come. Foreshadowing, you could call it.

Because this is New England, the fence travels uphill and down; only little bits of it are on the level. Although string lightheartedly imitates the contours of the land, boards have to be held in place, the angle of cut defined by pencil. Invariably, both ends of the boards want cutting. The eye wants readjustments despite the ruler. Sometimes bottom boards catch on hummocks, outcroppings, or earth bulges which must be shoveled out or the board rearranged. But let's say you've tacked up your whole top line for the day, you've stepped back, eyeballed and readjusted it. Oh, the hammering home! The joy and vigor of sending nails through hemlock into the treated four-by-four uprights. Such satisfying whacks, such permanence, such vengeance against the mass bustications of horses and heifers through the puny electric wire of yore. Visions of acres and acres of fences, field after field tamed, groomed, boarded in; that is the meaning of gluttony.

Finishing the fence—painting, staining, or applying preservative—requires the same constancy as the slow crafting of it. You put in your two hours a day, rejoice when rain interrupts the schedule and your Calvinist soul is permitted to tackle some other chore. Cleaning tack, for example, provides a pleasurable monotony compared to the servitude of the four-inch roller and the can of Noxious Mixture. In our case, it's composed of one-third diesel oil, one-third used crankcase oil, and one-third creosote. You are properly garbed to apply this Grade C syrup, wearing cast-off overalls, a battered felt hat, decayed boots, and thick neoprene gloves. You stand almost an arm's length away from the fence in order to get enough leverage so the mixture will penetrate wood grain—here tough, there smooth, here cracked and warty, there slick as a duck's feather. You invent methods for relieving the dreary sameness of the job. On one course you begin left to right, top to bottom, back to front. On the next you reverse the order. Sometimes you do all the undersides first, or all the backs. Sometimes you spring ahead, lavishly staining all the front-facing boards just to admire the dark wood lines dancing against the hummocky terrain of these young—yea, virginal—fields. The process gets you in the shoulder blades, later in the knees. You spatter freckles of the stuff on your protected body. Your protective eyeglasses are now freckled with iridescent dots. The stench of the mix permeates your hair, your gloved hands, becomes a way of life. You can no longer gain a new day without putting in your two hours staining board fences. More compelling than tobacco or alcohol, that addictive odor of char, of disinfectant, of grease pits. The horses follow you along the fence line, curious, but even the fresh-faced filly keeps a respectful distance from you and your repellent mixture.

A year later you sit atop the remnants of a six-foot-wide stone wall unearthed along the perimeter of number two field and look across to the remarkable pear tree that stands alone in the third and newest field. Behind you, the first field; behind it, the barn. Between fields, hedgerow and hickory trees, red pine and hemlock. An intermittent brook further defines the boundary between number one and number two. A tributary meanders at the foot of number three. Beyond, a lifetime of second-growth woodland awaits. In your mind's eye, an infinity of fenced fields recedes but never vanishes. And all the livestock of a lifetime safely graze.

SUMMER

Two Foals

I am writing in my journal in the blackness of the barn while waiting for a mare to foal. This page is illuminated by a sixty-watt bulb screwed into a mechanic's trouble light, which hangs from a nail over my head.

This spring, five horses live here at ground level in box stalls. Sawdust bedding is heaped in a bin roughly fifteen by six feet parallel to the last stall on the south side. This week I am sleeping in the bin on the levelled-out pile. Under me are a couple of foam pads left over from the children's camping experiences. Although it is the middle of May, the nights are cool and damp and I wear thermal longjohns inside my ancient sleeping bag.

It's a cozy situation, despite the faintly musty odor of old cotton batting. Abra and Cadabra, sister barn cats, sleep on my feet. I can check on the mare periodically by raising up on one elbow to peer over the partition. Although her milk-bag is full and hard, night after night she resists dropping her foal.

I view this as a contest of wills; she is determined to protect her privacy. I, on the other hand, am determined to witness the event. This mare lost her first foal a few years ago and no one was able to detect any abnormalities in the situation. The self-blame I assumed then is with me still.

This time I mean to stand by to rupture the sac, resuscitate the newborn, even to pull on a sterile obstetrical sleeve and reach in to free a stuck shoulder. I have never performed any of these heroic measures, but I have attended lectures and studied diagrams of malpositions until they are engraved on my retina.

In the meantime, I overhear every rustle, munch and snore. There is no resisting my surveillance. If the mare lies down, I wake up. When she lies down she sleeps with one foreleg cocked under her throat, pressing on the epiglottis (at least this is how I explain it to myself) and the snoring assumes epic proportions. Perhaps the giant in Jack and the Beanstalk snored this fiercely. Or Polyphemus, or one of Beowulf's monsters. The whole barn reverberates.

If the mare gets up from lying down, I wake up, too. I'm there on one elbow with my trusty flashlight to see if the situation is still static. In the aromatic dark our eyes meet, hers a burning, feral red. I wonder what she thinks of mine, which are not phosphorescent. It feels as if something wayward and telepathic is taking place between us. Floating ectoplasms would not surprise me. But at dawn the world rebegins. She is happy to have me on the spot. She puts her nose up over the top board and nickers in a soft way that suggests the cooings of large doves. She would like to be fed, she says.

I stagger up, fling open the long-defunct chest freezer, scoop out her two quarts of grain, sprinkle the top with the approved dietary supplement. Then, trailing my sleeping bag like Isadora's many scarves, I repair to my own bed across the road, confident the mare will not go into labor in daylight.

Tonight before I write in my journal, I read an essay by Anne Tyler in a group of essays, including one of my own, about our states of being as writers.* The aptness of her insight gives me goosebumps inside the musty sleeping bag. She speaks of having to divide the part of her that writes from the part that copes with everyday life. "Hewing our creative time in small, hard chips from our living time" is how Tyler puts it. Yes, oh yes, amen, sister!

The world thinks it's the other way around. People almost invariably have an image of the writer fixed at her desk, serene, uninterruptible, Olympian in her detachment. How orderly, how idyllic their fantasy. And how unattainable.

Anne Tyler is still wrestling with children's sudden high fevers, the vagaries of washing machine repairmen, and unannounced visits from Jehovah's Witnesses. I, whose children have grown and gone, have settled into a hillside farm out of sight or sound of neighbors. All this chaos is of my own devising. But it is the stuff of my life and I cannot make do without it.

The first mare's foal this spring came at two in the morning, although not quite in the prescribed fashion. Usually a mare in labor will act somewhat discomfited. She will pace, get up, lie down, perhaps permit herself a few grunts. She will at least rustle around in her stall. Suzy, my horse helper, who was foal-watching that week and sleeping so lightly that the local hoot owl roused her every night, heard no pre-

*Anne Tyler, "Still Just Writing." In *First Person Singular,* edited by Joyce Carol Oates (Princeton, N.J.: Ontario Review Press, 1983), p. 168.

monitory snufflings or sighs. What woke her was the sound of rushing water. She realized that the membranes had ruptured and buzzed Victor on the intercom. (Of course, I was out of town teaching a class, secure in the knowledge that the mare's udder consisted merely of two little pancakes. Thus we had days to go.)

By the time Victor had pulled on his jeans and sprinted across the road to the barn the little filly had emerged. The two horses lay quietly talking, exchanging little nuzzles and nickers. After ten minutes or so, according to my informants, the mare arose and licked her baby all over quite roughly. In another few minutes the little one was up and nursing. In biology this is called bonding, a purely instinctual performance.

I call it a miracle.

Some weeks ago, to a friend who is planning to visit, I announced the imminent arrival of two foals. Back came an enthusiastic but misguided letter: "Twins! How exciting! How did you find out you were expecting twins, ultrasound?"

I know I shouldn't resent this twitter of misinformation, but it always seems to me as ignorant as the city guests who ask if you are milking the yearling heifers. Someone has to explain to them that the heifers are virgins and that, like other mammals, a cow must be bred in order to give milk. It is odd indeed, but such logic has not crossed many an urban threshold.

People generally do not know how dangerous twinning is in the equine. Twin embryos usually spontaneously abort well before term. In some instances, one live twin is born and a second, often malformed, much smaller foal is delivered dead. The mare's uterus is not constructed to house two fetuses, but occasional live twin births do occur. These events are rare enough to warrant a newspaper article. Twin Standardbreds were dropped in New Jersey a few years ago at a major breeding farm. *The New York Times* carried their pictures, but the name of the mare was a closely guarded secret to protect her future as a broodmare. So the prospect of twins was something new to chew on, especially between one and three a.m. when I am vulnerable to severe twinges of meta-worry.

The day after the first foal slipped so effortlessly into the world, the second mare comes in from her loafing shed for the evening meal and spurns it. Since she is an exceptionally greedy eater, we know Her Time Has Come. I settle down quietly out of sight with a glass of wine and a good book.

The mare, while not distraught, is clearly restless. She lies down, gets up, lies down again. I can actually see the contractions rippling down her flanks. Her chest is patchy with sweat. Calmly, confidently, I wait.

Daylight wanes. The contractions vanish. The mare gets up, shakes herself, walks over to her feedbox and inhales every particle of her grain ration. She then proceeds to attack the fresh oat straw with which we have hastily and lavishly bedded her stall. (Straw for parturition is considered a safer, less septic medium. It is also extremely expensive, at least in New England—about twice the price of good hay.)

I sleep very well that night, subliminally aware of the engine of her digestion running as the mare casually chews her way through all the bedding.

The next evening the mare tucks into her grain with no hesitation, then vigorously turns her attention to a flake of hay. Mares are supposed to go off their feed before foaling, so I am feeling a little grim about matters. But wait! Something has happened. She is waxing—two little beads of colostrum have formed on her teats.

Authorities all agree on the significance of this signal. She will foal within the next twelve to twenty-four hours. Although she is simply hanging out looking relaxed and satisfied, Suzy and I agree to take turns checking the mare every ten minutes.

After several alternate trips to the barn we agree that nothing will happen before eight or nine p.m. The mare will wait for what is tritely referred to in mystery stories as "the cover of darkness."

Suzy goes off to wash her hair. I make another halfhearted trip across the road. No discernible difference. Suzy proceeds to dry her hair. I toss the salad. We are ready to sit down to supper: Suzy makes another sortie to the barn.

I hear her yelling before I see her racing back to the house. In eight minutes' elapsed time the mare has foaled and they are both on their feet.

So much for the "cover of darkness" theory. So much for my surveillance, sawdust nights, sterile obstetrical gloves. What we find is a wet, marbleized, wobbly baby. It bops from corner to corner, bumping into walls, feed tub, water bucket. For some dreadful minutes I think it may be brain-damaged. We hang onto it long enough to determine its gender—another filly!—and to saturate the navel stump with iodine. More than an hour passes before the little one is calm enough and hungry enough to find her way by trial and error to the mare's swollen udder.

The poor mare alternately nickers and squeals as that voracious mouth clamps onto her teats. Gradually, though, the stimulus of sucking relieves the fullness, and with it the pain. Suzy spends one last night on the sawdust pile to be sure the two have established a firm bond.

Now we have another miracle. This one is fawn-colored, going to be red chestnut, with a crooked white blaze running down her forehead, asymmetrical enough to suggest the map of South America.

What luck to have two fillies! On the family farm a colt presents problems. He has to be gelded, preferably before he is a year old, both to reduce the trauma of castration and to catch him before he is sexually mature enough to mount the mares. In the animal kingdom at least, the female of the species is prized for obvious reasons. She can be used to continue the bloodline. I am full of the mythology of frolicking foals, improved stock, generations to come.

The first week of fillies is one of cautious vigilance. We have two very protective mares, two insouciant foals. The later-born filly does not seem to distinguish readily between the two mahogany-colored maternal rumps and sometimes importunes the wrong mother. Neither mare will permit her baby to have anything to do with the other one. A certain amount of rushing around with ears back takes place. There are some imperious trumpetings to retrieve errant offspring. And I had forgotten how shrill the calls of foals can be, and how plaintively they nicker when momentarily misplaced.

Our pastures are so hilly that we have set aside our one almost-flat field especially for this first month out in the world. There is a bosky grove of pines at one end. The rest is wall-to-wall bromegrass and clover. Getting to it, though, requires negotiating a hilly stretch punctuated by water bars. These must seem like monumental hurdles to the young ones. Haltering and leading two skittish foals up this incline is a daily expedition into the Himalayas, accompanied only by our wise old Dalmatian, whom the mares trust.

Although they were born only two days apart, the physical difference between the fillies is marked. One is big, chesty, assertive, with a wonderful long stride. The other is refined, slender, spooky, and as fast as greased lightning. Now that they are turned out on these two acres, I am especially glad we had the foresight to reserve this field. Once in motion, it looks as though the foals can never stop short of the hemlock fence boards, but somehow they do.

Now, at the end of June, the mothers have resumed their former relationship. They graze side by side, frequently standing head to croup to take advantage of each other's fanning tail. The six-week-old babies lie down a lot, often out of sight behind the scrim of daisies and Indian paintbrush. At some magical moment two weeks ago, it was decreed that they could freely mingle. Now, unless thirsty or frightened, they ignore the dams and stay together. One is the hub of the wheel; the other races in circles around her. They touch noses, whinny, spin, and cavort. They crop grass together as best they can with their foreshortened necks, straining to reach the greenery between widely spraddled front legs. Perhaps a bird startles them, or the wind creaks an overhead branch and they are off again, doing pirouettes and piaffes.

I confess I am spending a lot of time hanging over the fence this summer. The ballet is endless, repetitious, aesthetically spectacular, and I never tire of it.

To be this happy, this content in a ravaged world, is to exist in an extreme state. "Oh, let there be nothing on earth but laundry," Richard Wilbur says in a poem extolling washday in Rome with linens flapping like banners from tenement windows. *Let there be nothing on earth but laundry* is now my shorthand for this precarious condition of happiness. The hay is not in, the garden barely planted, half of next winter's wood is still to be split and stacked. But this is the year of two fillies, two missed births with two happy outcomes. *Oh, let there be nothing on earth but laundry.*

Estivating — 1973

The reason I am keeping a journal this season of the hearings and the horses is to put down those "bits of the mind's string too short to use," as Joan Didion once said. Things tie themselves together with little quote marks and perhaps the string crosshatches itself into a statement in time, who knows? My son, scanning *The New York Times* one weekday morning when it was heavy with financial articles of the technical sort, complained, "not even anybody good died today" and I hang onto that phrase as it reflects the kind of stasis I am in, estivating here.

I came away from the city the first day of June,* no longer in the grip of one routine, promptly though voluntarily snared in another one, for my friend and neighbor across the

*At the time that this essay was written, the author and her husband were still weekend and summer residents. Three more years were to pass before they moved in year-round and life long.

valley has leased me two mares for the riding and gifted me with two foals* for the caring. Some impulse toward order propels me into the nonpermissiveness of animals to care for, a schedule to adhere to. I think I am afraid of too much latitude—how else could I handle such large blocks of time? As it is, I sleep less and more lightly than I have in years. One night the bay mare, for reasons of her own, took out a railroad tie and twenty feet of fence board. A week later, the colt and the filly, having spent several hours worrying the top slide board out of its double fixture, exploded out of the barn at two a.m. and we went barefoot flapping after them. They wanted only to be in the paddock with the mares, it seems. We want them stabled at night, thinking them too young and venturesome to roam. It is a return to the era of earaches and chicken pox and the nightmares of young children. Presumably, it serves some purposes, vague ones—the animal pleasure of touch, an aesthetic gratification—and it uses up some of my maternal obsessions. And is perhaps a way of hanging loose in between some more sustained efforts. Always the small terror of a prolonged block hovering just off stage, waiting to set in like an ice age. In any case, it makes me remember Orwell saying ". . . there has literally been not one day in which I did not feel that I was idling . . . as soon as a book is finished, I begin, actually from the next day, worrying because the next one is not begun and am haunted by the fear that there will never be a next one."

Noondays, I try to think up here in this boxy, pale blue room. I think of Virginia Woolf's aunt who did her the kindness of falling from her horse while riding out to take the air

---

*Weanlings, unrelated to the mares.

in Bombay and leaving her a legacy for life, enough for that room of one's own. The desk that I sit at in this room is an old oak piece left over from a schoolhouse when the century turned. It has a shallow pencil drawer and two sturdier deep ones and it stands on four unturned legs. Through the window it overlooks an equally unremarkable barn, once a dairy barn for fifty head of Holsteins. Years before our tenancy, an artist lived here and favoring the north light for his gloomy canvases—at least the ones he left behind are unremittingly dour in theme and muddy of color—he built an absurd sort of overhang from the haymow. It juts out like a Hapsburg jaw, looming halfway across the one-car-width dirt road that divides house and barn. I can sit here and watch swallows come and go through the gap tooth of an upper board where they coexist with the red squirrels. Yesterday, an owl, late awake in the mizzly weather, flapped his way in, presumably in search of mice. I hope he is snugly tenanted for a while, since he has a habit of hooting his way uphill tree by tree in the small hours announcing something. A very prepossessing paddock connects into the expired dairy farmer's dung heap, now leveled out and used as a shelter for the mares. Except they often prefer to stand out in a downpour, looking woebe-gone but cool.

From my window I can see the strawberry roan mare tearing up grass by its roots, munching dirt and all, swash-buckling the flies and mosquitoes with her bug-repellent–larded tail. Her coloring is rather like that of a redheaded woman, the freckled variety. This, I realize, stands for my four aunts, now deceased, who were always diminishing their spots with cocoa butter.

Privately, I call this mare Amanda and I am writing a

cycle of poems for her. She is a sensible and almost never petulant creature, on the enormous side (Aunt Harriet?) with feet as big as dinner plates and the girth of a California wine keg. A broad white blaze down her face lends her a look of continuous startle (Aunt Alma's plucked eyebrows?). And of course that voluptuous golden tail and mane, brillo consistency. She knots these by rubbing on the fence. We spend hours together. I do the combing and she, placidly, enjoys the small sensual tugs of the bristles. Until I was twelve I suffered two heavy plaits of hair, continually coming unbraided. "Stand still!" my mother would say. "Your part is as crooked as Ridge Avenue." Now my mother's hair is as thin and white as spun sugar, coaxed from a baby-pink scalp. This is the kind of reflecting that comes of combing.

Meanwhile, the Watergate unfurls its tattered length daily and we catch bits of it between barn and pond. It is a wondrous decadence, this daytime opéra bouffe, beaming in over the hills to this isolated spot. We worm the babies in the middle of John Dean's testimony and at last I see a connection. Although it makes me want to be sick, I count the nematodes in the little ones' shit—forty the first day, fifty-six the next. I am making sure.

Carless, two miles from town, we ride the horses down the back way, through the covered bridge, along the old railroad bed, and come out at the laundromat which was once a station stop on the B & M line. We tie them to the VFW flagpole, fifty yards from the general store. It seems a fitting use. When we remount, milk, flour, butter and beer in knapsacks, I see that Amanda has left a little pyramid on the lawn.

———◆———

Mornings, early, we go for long trips over corduroy and dirt roads that have lost their destinations, although the county area map still notes the burying grounds and sugar houses of a hundred years ago. It is chanterelle time, their dry yellow vases nicely visible in the woods at this height. It is like looking for butter. I remember Laurie telling me that in Provence if you want to go mushrooming you must start at daybreak or the other foragers will have picked the woods clean. Here, we can go all day loading our burlap saddlebags with fresh edibles, and not meet another person. It is a delicious depravity, feasting on our find—how far we are from the real world! What does the mushroom know? Only to open the hinges of its gills and shower down its blind spores— white, pink, rusty brown, or the good black of the inky caps. It corrects itself, this fruiting body, it is phototropic. Thanks to gravity, something will fall on fertile ground, though most stay stuck on the gills like words on a page. I suppose I mean that love is like this; as evanescent, as easily lost, as mindless, blind, instinctual. Or it is all a metaphor for the poem, the genesis of the poem as unexpected as the patient mushroom you come upon.

Today I order two hundred pounds of horse chow from the Feed and Grain Exchange in the next town. I do this by phone, apologetically, because I have no car and must ask for a delivery. The woman taking my twelve-dollar* order chats

* At this writing 100 pounds of mixed grain, 12 percent protein, sold for approximately six dollars. Fourteen years later, the price has appreciated less than any other commodity I can think of, including toilet paper and turpentine. Lo! The poor farmer.

with me, a long and cordial conversation between strangers who will likely never meet. Afterward, I think about the natural courtesy of it and all the city-surly bank clerks, taxi drivers, and cops who throw this moment into high relief.

Today, two startling finds: an enormous stand of ripe raspberries that fell off their stems into our pails, and yielded twelve jars of jam, and several fresh boletes of a kind I had never seen before. They matched in every way *Boletus mirabilis,* which is native to the Pacific Northwest. We ate them gratefully for supper, enfolded into omelets and praised the name and serendipity of their arrival. The mushroom passion freshens with me year by year. Too bad it is such an esoteric subject for Americans—each genus is as distinct as beet from rutabaga. A beet poem would speak its own universal, but a boletus poem? They are, of course, the toadstools in *Alice* and all those dreadful fairy books of my childhood, each with an elf underneath. Little children are taught to trample them on sight as something nasty to be eradicated. A pity. Once you have eaten wild mushrooms, the dull store-bought agaricus is a poor substitute. I think of Thoreau's "a huckleberry never reaches Boston." I pickle some mushrooms, string others with needle and thread and hang them to dry. Extras I sauté and freeze, but they are a pale imitation of the fresh-picked-and-into-the-pot ones.

This morning I hoed between the corn rows and thought up ways to foil the raccoons who will unerringly arrive with the first ripe ears. A transistor radio tuned to an all-night rock and roll station? Camphor balls and creosoted rope around the perimeter? One of my farmer neighbors claims that balls of newspaper between the rows will keep them off; they dislike the crackle. What to make of the picking and gathering in? One part thrift, one part madness; three parts inexplicable.

In Yeats's journal, the work sheets for "the fascination of what's difficult" contain these notes: "Repeat the line ending 'difficult' three times, and rhyme on bolt, exult, colt, jolt. One could use the thought of the wild-winged and unbroken colt must drag a cart of stones out of pride because it's difficult." ("I swear before the dawn comes round again / I'll find the stable and pull out the bolt.") But the domestication has got the better of me; lose half a garden and begin again. "Oh masters of life, give me confidence in something." Yeats again. So it seems I put my trust in the natural cycle, and bend to it. It is so far removed from self-improvement as to be an escape hatch. Nature pays me no attention, but announces the autonomy of everything. Here nothing is good or bad, but *is,* in spite of.

Herons

Two gentlemen from the Audubon Society arrived at our hill farm one July morning to see about the long-legged waders, *Ardea herodias*. They were armed with bug spray and hats and carried serious-size binoculars.

The Squire was insulating under the barn at the time, nailing chicken wire over fiberglass batts to guard against another seizing of the pipes in the laundry room next winter at thirty-five below. He emerged wearing cobwebs and pink fluff in his hair. Yes, of course, the Audubons. Late last April in a moment of euphoria he had called headquarters to report that we had sighted several great blue heron nests.

A large, leaky beaver pond lies athwart one of our secret trails, a single-file ribbon we've tramped on horseback to connect one lost woods road with another. It's a thriving affair with several active lodges and fifty or so dead trees standing sentinel in the middle. We had counted eight nests and possibly eleven young during the spring, and it seemed to us that this might be a notable number.

Herons

We are not what you would call serious birders, though we feed an assortment of hangers-on year round. In the winter we support upwards of forty evening grosbeaks. In summer we seem to specialize in goldfinches. This season a bluebird stopped by briefly in May, and a pair of Baltimore orioles is nesting in an apple tree below the barn. Some years ago we hosted three wild turkeys. If the Audubon Society rated its members by degrees of expertise the way the Pony Club does, we'd be D-1s, going for our D-2s.

Our callers were not, they regretted, horseback riders. It was too far to hike the whole way. After a little fussing over maps and logistics it was agreed that I would take them by four-wheel drive up the corduroy as far as possible. From that point we traveled by shank's mare.

I had forgotten to tell them it was a good climb, and, as they were gentlemen of a certain age, we paused every hundred yards or so for a breather. Although we had all introduced ourselves, their names had been swallowed up in the discussion over alternate routes and mudhole avoidance. In my head I called them the Messrs. Eagle and Osprey, as the former appeared single-minded and rapacious of vision, the latter a little smaller and nice about sharing his eyepiece.

It was Osprey who kept identifying birdsongs as we paused along the trail. Only the most common ones, he said modestly. In a three-minute interval he reeled off chestnut-sided warbler, wood pewee, oven bird, red-eyed vireo, wood thrush and scarlet tanager. Chickadee, nuthatch, blue jay, crow, white-throated sparrow and robin were beneath notice, of course. These are calls even a D-1 can recognize.

Things were quiet at the pond site except for the territorial outpourings of a couple of unexpected redwing blackbirds. Some swallows were swooping, crosshatching the water, gathering up insects. Judging from the swarm of mosquitoes that had attached itself to us, the birds were finding easy pickings.

Eagle distanced himself from us a little and set about scanning the ramparts. Osprey and I visited back and forth sharing his binoculars. There were eleven easily visible nests in ten trees; rumpled, every-which-way nests of sticks and mud and dried grasses. They were built into the crosspieces of branch stubs very close to the tops of dead pines. Some of these trees stood forty feet above the water. Wearing their slatternly nests they looked like the frontispiece of an old children's book called *Der Struwelpeter*—"Slovenly Peter"—that I grew up on. A few of the nests were so flimsy and haphazard that it seemed they would not last the season. Others were sizable platforms six feet or so across, and thick enough to withstand a lot of preflight flapping around.

My favorite tree, the apartment complex, had in its top nest two visible gray lumps of babies, probably recently hatched. On the lower level, eight or ten feet down, three rangy youngsters waited to be fed. They lined up in blue-gray profile, perfectly still, silhouetted against the watercolor sky.

As the clouds scudded past, an eerie half-sun showed itself. The light had a tentative quality to it, glinting on the drying stick piles of beaver lodges and raising little sequins of glitter from the still-wet marsh grasses. It was a primal moment. We could have been—we were!—anywhere in time or place.

No wonder Chinese artists were so attracted to the heron as a subject. You can see how, with a line here, an interrupted line there, here a thick curve, there a thin one, you have it: the sharp, pointed bill, slicked-back head plume, slender neck, rounded shoulders, knobby leg joints. John Ciardi used to tell a story to would-be poets about the ancient Chinese emperor who commissioned an artist to paint a heron on the palace wall. The artist bowed respectfully and backed out of the royal presence. A year passed, during which we surmise the artist practiced furiously in his sketchbook. When he returned with his paintpot and brush, he walked up to the blank wall and without hesitation created a magnificent heron in three brush strokes. What was important, Ciardi explained, making an analogy to the poem, was the source of his impromptus.

One impromptu source appeared just then out of the west, coming in like a plane laboring to let down its landing gear. I was surprised to see how clumsily the bird's legs trailed out behind the body, yet how adroitly the heron reversed the angle of its body and gained the edge of the nest. The fledglings, even before he or she landed—it isn't easy to distinguish between the sexes, although the male is said to be somewhat larger—set up a clatter like prisoners beating on the bars of their cages with bed slats. It is a wooden-metallic noise that sounds machine-made. These rattles, bangs and chugs persisted until the parent had emptied its craw and flown off to recuperate atop a nearby unoccupied tree.

By then, another adult had arrived to deal with another clutch of importunate young ones, and the clatter of bed slats arose again. Then another, and another. For a little while it seemed as though the sky held nothing but great blue herons.

Eagle by now had repaired to a little tongue of land that licked out into the pond and was alternately looking through his eyepiece and scribbling in his notebook. He lamented several times that he had not packed along his telescope, and I was sorry, too. I would have loved to have had an even closer look at the feeding program. But, given the uphill trek, a telescope might have been the camel's straw.

We all reapplied bug spray and stood around swatting

several minutes more to see if we could tell what was being fed. Frogs, salamanders, snakes, fish—a high-protein diet, whatever was being disgorged from those grownup craws. Dragonflies are considered a choice morsel, as are unwary mice, shrews, or other little land creatures.

The raucous breakfast sounds were audible all the way back to the woods road as we departed. Perhaps the birds were more active because the preceding days had been so stormy. It must have been hard for the parents to find food in monsoonlike rains. I, who am a coward about electric storms, remembered with a shudder the violence of the last series and thought how the sky must have looked from the mizzenmasts of those nests in the pond. In that primal setting where growth and decay concur, the jags of lightning could have signaled the end of the world, the start of a new one.

Herons raise only one clutch a season, and that one takes a long time. They start nesting in April. Most of the fledglings get launched in August, although days in the nest may vary between sixty-some and ninety. Many of the young will not make it to maturity. It was Eagle who told me there are varying levels of intelligence in the avian world within any given species. Some of these youngsters may not be able to learn how to fend for themselves. Some will not master frogging or fishing on their own and will quite simply starve to death. Herons have been known to strangle on an oversize fish. Some die in freak accidents involving power lines or fences. Others fall prey to predators like fisher cats or raccoons, or even an enterprising coyote.

It is hard to think of losing as many as half of this batch through Darwinian selection. On the other hand, every farm pond within a ten-mile radius will be pirated, stripped clean of fish and amphibian life if they all survive.

We reported back to the Squire, who was torn between admiration for the heron rookery and proprietary feelings for the two hundred brookie fingerlings in his own little pond. He will put a transistor radio on the shore as the first heron swoops in. More likely, though, it will work about as well as it does to fend off raccoons in the corn. Two cheers for Nature, which will have the final say.

Silver Snaffles

The best present of my childhood, a British storybook called *Silver Snaffles*, by Primrose Cumming, arrived on my tenth birthday. In this fantasy tale, a little girl walks through the dark corner of a draft pony's stall into a sunlit world where articulate ponies with good English country-squire manners and highly individual personalities give lessons in equitation and stable management to some eager, horseless youngsters. After several instructive episodes the story culminates in a joyous hunt staged by the foxes themselves, who are also great conversationalists. Jenny, launched as a rider, learns that she is to be given a pony of her own. Now she must relinquish her right to the magic password and to the dark corner of Tattles's stall, through which she has melted every evening into a better world. I thought it the saddest ending in the whole history of literature.

By this age I had already begun to ride—an hour a week, one dollar an hour—on one of those patient livery horses who put up with the clumsiness of the novice. A year or two later, when I could wield a manure fork and manage a full-size

wheelbarrow, I began to learn something about stable management. It didn't especially matter to me whether I rode or
not; I was happy just to be in the presence of horses. I wanted
to inhale them, and I wanted them to take me in. Days that
I wasn't allowed to walk two miles to the rental stable, I
skulked above stairs and reread *Silver Snaffles*.

Eventually, I wore this book out with ritual rereadings;
somehow it disappeared from my life. When, forty-odd years
later, I assumed my duties at the Library of Congress, it oc-
curred to me that *Silver Snaffles* was undoubtedly housed in
that enormous repository of knowledge. The day I found it
in the cavernous, dusty stacks, I sat down on the marble floor
and turned the familiar pages in disbelief. The book was real,
after all! Then I carried it up to the Poetry Room that overlooks the Capitol and the Mall and read the story all over
again, savoring the parts I had remembered verbatim. While
serious affairs of state were being conducted only a few hundred
yards away, I patted the sturdy, faded blue cover and wept.

I think I was crying for my lost childhood, but I'm still
not sure. The profound, cathartic effect of the book was not
assuaged for me by Jenny's acquiring a pony of her own.
Nothing would compensate for that loss of innocence, the un-
worldliness that had enabled her to speak the password and
walk into a kingdom of virtue and honor. There, all the ponies were Platonic philosopher-kings, and the children, their
willing pupils, rose with pure hearts through the ranks of Be-
coming to the heightened state of Being represented by well-
mucked stalls, well-ridden and chatty equines, and steaming
bran mashes.

At this remove, I can now understand my fascination
with the text. The deprivation that I felt when the heroine
was denied continued access to Paradise was the loss of something I can only call interspecies communication. *Pace,* Anna

Freud; *pace,* D. H. Lawrence; this bonding, I believe, lies at the heart of horse fever for any age or gender.

Interaction with the horse takes place on several levels. Physical communication is foremost. You learn its body language and it learns to respond to a body language you use to ask for changes in gait, direction, and body frame. You may spend weeks and weeks going around the dressage ring or beaten track in your pasture, riding a stiff, unbalanced, green horse, thinking *round, round,* and asking with your body aids for flexion, for bending, for the horse to use its hind legs, to track up under its body, to come onto the bit instead of lagging behind it. And then one day there is a little breakthrough. For two or three strides you and your horse move in absolute harmony. Later, another breakthrough and another. You are ecstatic. The horse is pretty happy, too. He/she has understood you, made the effort, developed the supporting musculature, and goes forward confidently, in balance. From this two-way exchange evolves a shared precision, a shared joy in fluidity of motion, rhythm and cadence not unlike the delight an athlete takes in executing, for example, figures on skates, or completing a slalom course on skis or performing intricate high dives. We have, blessedly, an atavistic need to let our bodies speak. To achieve a bonding with a horse you have raised and schooled from its gawky weanling stage, to arrive at control without exploitation, to work toward new goals that mean stretching limits for both horse and rider is to employ that body language, and to do so with equestrian tact. Like poetic tact, also based on a sense of touch, it is arrived at only gradually and with self-discipline.

Horses, like people, enjoy enlarging their scope. Horses asked only to perform the same routine day after day grow dull, bored, apathetic. Faced with new fields, a variety of trails, different cross-country courses and dressage rings, the supple, athletic, healthy horse takes pleasure in meeting the challenge.

Growth and change without brutality, achieving goals by skilled effort on both parts, depend on interspecies communication. At the risk of sounding sexist—some wonderful trainers and handlers are male—I profoundly believe that women work best with problem horses. (This is not the same thing as riding them best over seven-foot *puissance* walls in Madison Square Garden.) Women's empathy, subtlety, ability to read the nuance of difference that leads to change; women's gift of timing; women's instinct for nurturing, all contribute to their considerable successes, for example, in the large Thoroughbred and Standardbred breeding-farm operations; in the show ring; as exercise riders, grooms, and jockeys in the racing world; and as instructors at levels ranging from the local day-camp riding program to training establishments like Morven Park or the Potomac Horse Center.

Clinics I have attended, featuring a holistic approach to behavioral problems in a variety of performance horses, from Olympic contenders to backyard ponies, attract audiences that are 90 percent female. Somehow the notion of improving performance by developing a trusting partnership between horse and human elicits a readier response from women than from men. Old attitudes die hard; the macho concept of muscling a horse into submission still has its adherents.

Granted, many elements enter into the human passion for horses, and developing sexuality may be one of these. But the old stereotype about girls and horses has always seemed to me too facile to be trusted. For one thing, it does not take into account that the girl-horse affection is much more an East Coast phenomenon than a Western one. As you move into Colorado, Montana, Utah, and so on, you encounter a greater ratio of boys struck with the same fever. In a culture where the cow pony represents not only the freedom to explore space, but also the means to develop such working skills as cutting and roping and such recreational skills as rodeo riding or barrel-racing, males are in the majority. Eastern pony clubs and 4-H horse groups have been for the most part the purview of mothers, much as Little League has belonged for the most part to competitive fathers.

I further mistrust the Freudian concept because it does not adequately explain the substantial number of adult females who, despite their comfortable adaptation to sex roles involving marriage and child-rearing, continue to lease, own, care for, ride and/or raise horses. Some of us even do so in collusion with riding husbands, who are also unabashed nurturers and can be found pitching hay, sweeping up, and otherwise taking an active part in horsekeeping and riding.

I do not blink the fact that the horse often comes into a young girl's life at a time when she feels a need to take control in some measure of what is essentially an uncontrollable environment. The key factor is that an animal's responses can be counted on. When all else shifts, changes and disappoints, the horse can remain her one constant.

I asked Julia, my favorite twelve-year-old working visitor, why she loves riding horseback. These are her unrehearsed responses. "It gives you a sense of freedom. You're sort of out of touch because you're higher up than everybody else." And then she added, "Taking care of horses makes you feel good because you're making somebody else [sic] feel good. It's sort of a comforting feeling when you get done [with the evening barn chores] because you've put them away and you know you've made them feel cozy and secure."

The bond with horses, no matter its origin, becomes at some stage functionally autonomous. However it began, it is

enjoyed ultimately for its own worth.   Why else do I trudge
through four feet of snow and ice at below-zero temperatures,
winter after winter, to tend a barn full of mares and foals?
Intrinsic worth is what keeps me creosoting fences at the peak
of blackfly season, when merely to speak out of doors is to
inhale swarms of the nasty, biting gnats.   In summer heat waves
when the horses doze in cool stalls all day and are turned out
to graze all night, the barn must be cleaned at nine p.m.,
dinner guests or no.   In the searing electrical storms that pounce
in July and August, when fear of lightning striking in the open
pastures hurries me out to round up the scattered group, intrinsic worth keeps me going.   Under my breath I may mutter, "Virtue is its own reward, and that's all it is," a dictum
offered by the poet Howard Nemerov, but clearly I would not
have it otherwise.   And in the fall, when mosquitoes and deerflies wane and woodland trails are carpeted with alternating
patches of pine needles and still-bright leaves, intrinsic worth
mingles with all the sweetness of delayed gratification.

"The Horse," Gervase Markham wrote in 1614, "will take
such delight in his keeper's company, that he shall never approach him but the horse will with a kind of cheerful or inward neighing show the joy he takes to behold him, and where
this mutual love is knit and combined, there the beast must
needs prosper and the rider reap reputation and profit."

Cheerful or inward neighing is what I would cross-stitch on
a sampler, if I were assigned to work one, as my mother was.
Hers read, in the astonishingly even stitches of a twelve-year-
old, *He maketh me to lie down in green pastures.*   An appropriate
piety, under the circumstances.

Getting into the Register

"Every grain of barley given to a horse," it is written in the Koran, "is entered by God in the Register of Good Works." Getting into the Register according to that dictum has been one of the prevailing obsessions of my life.

I like to think that my obsession serves a larger good: Living with horses reminds us daily of our place in nature. The process of tending them, training, riding, or driving them establishes a direct tribal link with our collective past. In our grandparents' and great-grandparents' era the biological symbiosis between horse and human was a vital one. My own grandfather in rural Virginia, an estimable man I never met, took his entire family back and forth by rockaway and dog cart each autumn between somnolent Radford and bustling Roanoke, a distance of some forty miles. My mother, who is now eighty-three, remembers those days more vividly than these. I think warmly of my great red-bearded ancestor as I buckle on the filly's backpad and crupper and place her in the shafts. I know what I am doing: I am taking my rightful place in the continuum.

Getting into the Register

Even in my own childhood in suburban Philadelphia it was still a horsy world. Milk vans, bread vans, and open-backed garbage wagons were drawn by good chunky drays. "What has four wheels and flies?" went the favorite conundrum of my first-grade class.

The junkman reciting his mournful litany of "Rags? Any old rags? Any old bottles, papers, rags?" roamed the neighborhood with his elderly gelding. From time to time another entrepreneur, the clothes-prop peddler, could be heard traversing the same route. "Clo's-prop! Clo's-prop! Hang 'em up, poke 'em up, clo's-prop!" he chanted in synchrony with the deliberate, flat-footed walk of Sorry, his retired racing trotter. They named him Sorry because he was always sorry he lost, the story went.

The milkman's Nelly, on the other hand, seemed entirely happy in her work as she ambled from one side of the street to the other, stopping only at the entryways of subscribers to Supplee-Biddle's home delivery service. I marveled at her intelligence and was often on hand at that primitive hour of morning with sugar lumps I had filched from my mother's pantry.

But the happiest hours of my preschool life—if the combination of aesthetic delight and intense yearning that governed my secret life can be considered happy—were those spent in Fairmount Park idolizing the elite beasts of the mounted Guard. In common with the cavalry of yore, each man was responsible for his own horse. Each horse shone as if waxed and polished. The Guards' tack was immaculate, the horses' manners exemplary. Affable if condescending, man and mount allowed a child to worship at stirrup level.

The first horse I rode was named Charlie. He belonged to that legion of unsung heroes, the school horses. If there is a heaven, surely it is full of these patient creatures who for years carried on their backs the timid and inept, the eager and awkward. There was no arena or outdoor ring then at the top of McCallum Street, where Ross-Del's Riding Academy verged on the Wissahickon Woods. Bob Ross simply boosted me aboard the saddle and taught me—and dozens of other daughters of the middle class—how to post by riding closely enough alongside so as to grasp me firmly under the elbow.

It seemed humiliating to me at age eight to go forth attached to the riding master by lead shank and elbow, but I was not released from this bondage for some time. Later in my equestrian career, I earned free rides in exchange for all manner of muckings-out, groomings and tack cleanings. Had the ratio been fifty hours of drudging to one hour in the saddle it would have seemed a fair rate of exchange to me.

Twenty-five years later, my old fervent wish in hand, I went shopping for a horse. Nothing stood between me and my basic skills but a horse-hungry eleven-year-old daughter. It was February in New Hampshire's Upper Valley. The horses that passed through the weekly auction were, for the most part, a sad horde. Many were for sale because they had grown too expensive to feed or were in poor condition in other, less obvious ways. Dozens of tatterdemalions were trotted through the drafty arena that Saturday night while the audience in the grandstand alternately eyed the proceedings and dipped into picnic baskets for liquid fortification against the chill.

Although it was an education to watch the dealers in action, our first two trips netted us nothing but frustration. On the third excursion, accompanied by a horse-wise friend, we sighted two dapple-gray ponies a little on the thin side, but nicely put together. We went round to their pen and inspected them from all angles, finally selecting the larger of the two as having the greater potential. My friend reported that he had the deeper chest and the kinder eye, subtleties that then eluded me. They were grade animals, but had the look of Welsh ponies crossed with Arab. To my chagrin, when they came on the block the auctioneer announced that these green-broke, full-blood brothers, ages three and four, were only for sale as a pair.

Hasty consultation. What would we do with two of them? On the other hand, why not two? Two for company, two riders, tea for two. In slightly less time than it takes to tell, we acquired both Starlight and Stardust for $330 (the year was 1962, the year of a different dollar) and a verbal promise not to separate them. Their former owner, a Maine farmer, told us he had traded a tractor for them the year before. Disdained by his adolescent sons in favor of car engines, they had languished in his back pasture.

I arrived home elated in the frosty small hours. My sleepy mate, who had grown resigned to my Saturday-night defections, roused long enough to ask, "Did you buy a pony?" "No," I said, waiting with relish until he had rolled over and reclosed his eyes. "I bought two of them."

Dusty and Star shared one box stall. They stood always with the neck of one hung tenderly over the other's. From a distance they looked something like Doctor Doolittle's push-mepullyu gone a bit askew.

No one had ever done these ponies ill. Their view of the human race was a sunny, inquisitive one. Schooled, groomed, and outfitted, they went off to Pony Club rallies, local horse shows, and for long, lazy hacks in the woods. Somewhat underhorsed but happy in the one family saddle, I rode the larger pony and my daughter larruped along bareback on the thirteen-hand smaller one.

Six years later when the equestrian daughter went off to college, we sold the grays, again as a pair, and kept track of their destinies for quite a while. Dusty went on to take any number of blue ribbons for his new young rider, and Star, whinnying anxiously whenever he lost sight of his big brother, posed for pet pony pictures.

I am never good at leave-taking. What I remember most vividly of that era of the dapple grays is the act of driving down the highway in a September torrent behind the trailer bearing our ponies away. Through the blur of inadequate windshield wipers and a spate of tears I steered wholly by the polestar of their two red tail bandages.

Today, all six stalls in our barn are full. Only two of us—my husband and I—are in residence to ride them. This way madness lies, we agree. But who goes and who stays? On our own now, without a cooler head to chide us, we seem able only to acquire horses, not to disperse them. Maybe it was all predestined, this gradual accretion of horses. Surely by now we are firmly inscribed in the Register.

FALL

Wintering Over

A woman creeps on all fours through a squash patch in mid-September seeking out the late bloomers. The species is called spaghetti squash. Loosely ovoid, pallid green at first, yellowing as it seasons and toughens for winter keeping, it can be boiled, baked, or fried. No matter what culinary approach she takes toward it, the squash concludes as stringy. Seed catalogs have made a virtue of its stubbornly fibrous nature and advertise it as a noncaloric vegetable pasta.

Frost is predicted for tonight. She will cover the tomatoes with an assortment of discarded bed sheets and tablecloths, first setting out pans of water between the plants, for water acts in some perfectly logical scientific way she does not understand to keep the temperature up. It is her annual aim to hold the fruit on the vines until October. Since they live near the top of a hill overlooking the river valley and her tomatoes grow on a south slope along the foundation stones of the house, it is not an unreasonable ambition.

Her son, rattling up the hill in his ten-year-old Dodge,

pronounces that it is time to mow the truck. If he had helped
his father more vigorously, the pickup truck would not still
hunker on the grassy strip by the barn. The manure in the
back, destined last April for the garden located still farther up
the hill where the terrain yields a flat and sunny area, has long
since put up a fine crop of weeds and grasses. The boy and
his father are intermittently repairing the brake line. Each
redress on occasional weekends seems to result in another leak
farther along the line. The son has lost interest, he is not
cause-oriented; the young, remarks his father, want instant
gratification. He, on the contrary, loves his recalcitrant old
truck as fiercely as if it were a runaway.

Her mare is a dangerous runaway. She must recognize
this fact of their lives much as one might be forced to acknowledge an alcoholic mother or a retarded child. Therefore
of course she does not love her mare the less, but more. She
is a rescuer by temperament. Horses one cannot reform are
sent, in the country colloquialism, to the canner's. Rather
than reduce her mare to dog food, she sends her to be bred.
In the third estrus, the mare settles. Gravely and perfectly,
the matter is settled, for impending motherhood is said to
exert a calming influence on the flightiest mares. Like many
folk sayings, it sounds dubious and sexist.

The woods are fecund with mushrooms. Atop the settled mare each morning she rides along familiar trails made
surprising by the emergence of parasols and puffballs, hen-of-
the-woods, coral, and oysters. Each time she dismounts to
pick a treasure the mare sinks her teeth gratefully into a clump
of ferns, although ferns are not thought to be a respectable
fodder. In this manner they proceed into the hills until the
saddlebags are full. Yesterday in the village, casually gracing
a lawn and imitating split-seamed baseballs, three brain puff-

balls appeared. In this week's newspaper, a time-lapse series of photographs of a giant puffball which had burst the asphalt driveway leading to the Emersons's garage usurped the front page. Coming home she passes a pine log that has lain for years along the dirt road. Today, growing at forty-five-degree angles of inclination, two dog stinkhorns. *Phallus impudicus,* the handbook designates them. They are, in outline and dimension, exact Andy Warhol replicas. Is this nature's joke on art? And what of the force that drives the puffball upward against bewildering odds, against the counterforce of gravity reinforced by bitumens pressing down? Mother Seton has just been canonized for curing, among other ills, a documented case of leukemia. Isn't the puffball's defiance of technology a profane miracle?

She goes to an illustrated lecture on the care and management of the broodmare. It is given in the local high school by an apple-cheeked veterinarian who appears to be sixteen years old. Facts strike her as electrons bombard the nucleus of the atom. She learns, for example, that there are three criteria for breeding a mare back in the foal heat, the prime one being that the afterbirth weigh at least fourteen pounds and that it separate from the uterus of the mare within two hours of parturition. Colored slides accompany this information. The afterbirth, a tattered shawl of membranous blue streaked with red blood and luminous white stripes of tissue, hangs out of the vulva of a bay mare. The woman is the mother of three children; she has, in her own mother's quaint phrase, been to the well three times. Still, she is startled by a drawing of a uterus full of foal. Diagrams of wrong presentations assault her. Fetuses are portrayed rump-first, head-first but with front legs drawn back like fish fins, upside down, and sideways-wedged. Here, a mare who delivers standing up must be attended, else the foal will fall to the floor and the placenta sever prematurely, draining away one-sixth of the foal's blood supply. She makes a list of items to have in readiness: a Fleet enema, a solution of iodine to swab the umbilical cord (tear, do not cut), a syringe for the tetanus toxoid. She learns more than she ever wanted to know. The pregnancy is a commitment, from this there is no drawing back. When her mare comes to term this spring she will probably sleep in the barn. She hears the testimonies of others in the class who have spent three, twelve, sixteen nights on army cots outside their gravid mares' stalls. She feels reassured. She is part of a hardy band, a secret cell, an underground of true believers.

When the boy comes up the hill in his red Dodge Dart this September morning it is to see his sister, visiting from Europe where she lives. She is three years his senior and from the time he crept across the kitchen floor to paddle in the dog's water dish and she retrieved him, they have had a mythic bond. Now he is six feet tall, elegantly slender, with the sky-blue eyes of a newborn. A handlebar mustache mutes the fullness of his lower lip while giving his face a gently melancholic, if not world-weary air. He is twenty-two. His sister, although gracefully constructed, is five feet, one inch. So much for genetic similarities.

The mother watches them embrace. Camouflaged, she can afford to conduct some meticulous noticing. They are perfect with their four arms and four legs of mismatched lengths, and their laughter overlaps perfectly. Arms entwined like schoolchildren or young lovers, they leave the sun and go indoors. But the afterimage stays, it is as still as ectoplasm, and she can go on seeing them as long as she likes from her dog-squat in the squash patch.

Through two changes of equinox the truck has sustained

a flat tire. Not Liquid Wrench nor Naval Jelly nor an entire bottle of Coca-Cola will loosen the rusted lugs. The brake line, the clutch linkage, the little problem with the carburetor have all yielded this day to the double onslaught of father and son. Now they are going to pull the wheel loose with the tractor. Its engine starting up intensifies the chugging of red squirrels who claim overlapping territories in the abandoned apple trees. Nuts rain down unheard from the shagbark hickories and three parasol mushrooms, *Lepiota procera,* of seven, nine, and nine-and-one-half-inch diameters, wait to be found in the same upland grove as last year.

The woman is wearing her farmer pants, bib overalls with cretonne curtain patches where the cloth has worn through. Her son would prefer a mother who dressed in matching beige sweaters and skirts and a single strand of pearls. He would banish yogurt from her refrigerator, horses from her pasture, and yoga from her Tuesday nights. Stress is a physiologic response inappropriate to a situation. Adrenal production rises, muscles bunch in readiness, even the body's coagulation chemistry stands by in case of open wounds. In yoga class on Tuesday nights on a mat in the dank basement of the school that was built in the village ten years after the Civil War, she learns to breathe away stress. She goes through the multiple positions of Sun Worship, she assumes the Cobra, Fish, and Child poses. Her shoulder stands strengthen the lower back and tone up the organs that hang within the abdominal cavity although she is unclear about their relative positions. The instructor's script is banal, relying heavily on images of waves on a beach or clouds in the sky. The beneficial claims made for yoga are possibly ridiculous, she does not believe in astral projection or transcendental processes, but she slips away each week during the meditation period. That is to say, she loses contact. Possibly she dozes off? Whatever it is, it refreshes.

Her son does not like to come upon her practising her shoulder stands. He finds this position ungainly for a woman in middle age. Between mothers and sons the way is slippery. Her lower back aches right now and she slides one hand inside the loose waist of the overalls to massage the sore part, the lifting and bending fulcrum beaten hollow daily by her will. There is still goldenrod at the field's edge. Overhead, an afternoon of calmest blue. The swamp maples are turning already; she thinks of them as cowards. She would hold summer on the stalk another month at least. This was the time of year he traditionally came down with the croup, the little one they wintered over so painfully those early years with the kettle and the smell of tincture of benzoin in the room. His sister braved the steam to play checkers with him, or Fish or Old Maid. They ate fig newtons and the crumbs migrated between the sheets.

Even as the woman suffers these irrefutable nostalgias, three heifers and a young steer with a bald face crash about in the underbrush below the paddock. They have been loose all summer foraging through pockets of lost meadows that the woods enclose and wandering down networks of old logging roads. This mild autumn afternoon, driven perhaps by thirst and a longing for grain, they show themselves. The heifers are Jerseys. At careless first glance they are taken for deer, a prospect that startles. Having survived without human ministrations for several months, all are skittish. Even cornered, soothed with shakes of grain in the bucket, they have a disconcerting way of wheeling abruptly and clattering off into the scrub growth. More than an hour passes before they are penned. The heifers have vaccination tags in their ears. A mile or so clockwise, then counterclockwise about the paddock and the son wrestles one of them still enough so that his sister can call out the number. The veterinarian's wife runs it through her file and locates the appropriate dairy farmer, some fifteen miles distant. He is a man lackadaisical about his fences and his watering trough and unperturbed about his missing animals. Just at nightfall, his barn chores completed, he drives up the hill with his helper in the livestock truck. There was five run off, he insists. Three heifers and two beeves, run off last May, five in all. He does not accuse. Still, his statement sets in motion a new hypothesis after he has safely gone. They could have closeted the steer, at least, in the upper pasture and wintered themselves a good supply of steaks.

In truth, then, one steer has not survived his freedom. The woman sees him down somewhere in deep woods, trapped in a tangle of old barbed wire or fallen into an abandoned well. The others rush off, cattle fashion, from danger. She has a vision of that slow death. Indeed, she will come upon the skeleton one year hence, still wearing tags of its hide and pearl chips of cartilage. It is stretched on its side as if it had died in its sleep. Her horse will shy harshly from the mound that says mildly on the air, *carrion*.

They make a late supper after the excitement. The air has sharpened since sunset. An almost full moon slips up over the next hill. Both woodstoves are going, popping their cheeks from time to time. Outdoors, the tomato plants under their old bed sheets have taken on the outlines of white dinosaurs. It is all in vain. Nothing green can be had in trade this night. The horses sleep standing up, silently growing their winter coats as a hard frost rides in leaving a trail of white prints on the grass, the rooftop, the forgotten handbook of mushrooms left open to dog stinkhorn.

The Country Kitchen

Conjure up the country kitchen on a hard winter evening, the thermometer falling inexorably, so says the weather report, toward twenty degrees below zero. An hour ago in four p.m. twilight the animals came willingly into the barn to dry bedding, fresh water, sweet feed, and hay. A light snow had begun to swirl through the air in dry eddies. What comfort to slide the latches closed, whistle slavish dog and disdainful cat uphill into the heart of the house! They lie down together on their square of folded rug next to the cooking stove, hostilities suspended until daybreak.

Across the way, where a wall might logically set living room apart from kitchen, homemade vegetable soup thaws on the woodstove. On the hearth, twice-risen loaves of bread rest before being baked. No barrier separates living space from the food and general-activities center of the country house. Indeed, under pressure from a new way of life in which radiant heat from woodburning stoves must circulate unimpeded by dividers, virtually every house with a chimney today has abandoned the closed-door imperative of the high-technology kitchen.

My grandfather was fond of repeating the old saw: "from shirt-sleeves to shirt-sleeves in three generations." In a sense, the country kitchen bears him out. The second generation, only lately freed from the drudgery of dairy or truck farm, moved to city apartments and hurled itself into creating surgical kitchens full of glistening white appliances that disappeared into walls. In those sterile fastnesses it was easy to believe that the best food came in cans and was to be dealt with stealthily. The residue, full of dangerous bacteria, was whisked away.

In that era, cooking smells were believed to taint our higher faculties with a lower-class cabbaginess. For want of a separate room in which to consume foods, the eating area was screened by a series of ingenuities from the somehow prurient doings that took place between sink, refrigerator and stove. Remember the dining areas barricaded by latticeworks of lath up which crawled a sickly ivy? The breakfront dividers full of dusty knickknacks? The trompe l'oeil murals depicting distant, faintly Greco-Roman, landscapes? Whoever prepared the meals in those narrow, cramped outposts behind the façade was hidden as in a confessional from whoever ate them. Sinner was shielded from saint, as it were, in a curious reversal.

Now we have come full circle back to our roots, back to the land. We have leaped out of the closet into the eat-in kitchen. Now we revel in pots and pans depending from hooks over the stove, in garlic and onion braids festooning the window, dried-mushroom necklaces decorating the rafters. Basil, chives and parsley sit in pots on the sill. The inglorious potato rests mutely mounded in its bright plastic display box. Overhead, citrus fruits grow juicier at room temperature in their hanging baskets. We are no longer ashamed of appetite and odor. The kitchen has become the center of our house-pride.

Consider the democracy of the country kitchen as opposed to the scullery mentality of the separatist kitchen. A popular television ad used to show, speeded up, how many times a day the refrigerator door was opened in the average household of four. Think how many daily transactions take place in the country kitchen. How many feet enter, cross, and leave it from first light to bedtime, year-round. The farrier comes in, after shoeing, for a cold drink in summer, hot coffee in winter. The vet, celebratory after seeing to the broodmare and hours-old foal, admits he has had no breakfast. A neighbor walks up to use the phone to alert other abutters that three of his beefers have broken out. The goat's-milk person calls, seeking new clients. The county agent is checking earthen dams in our area. Chimney sweeps, Jehovah's Witnesses, woodlot assessors, a would-be buyer to try out the filly, the ancient and laconic man who stops by every summer to inquire after ginseng roots, all begin or end their visit in the kitchen. In one season the kitchen is to get warm in; in another, it's for cooling off. Much of our hospitality involves either the cold or the hot drink. All manner of small gifts go out from the country kitchen's larder—maple syrup, pickles, jams or jellies, dried herbs in little jars; even dried wild mushrooms for the knowledgeable or trusting.

In winter the kitchen table lends itself to Scrabble games. Between plays, family members are exhorted to pick nutmeats from hickories or butternuts. How else will these tedious tasks be done? The kitchen table is the logical place to pore over the new seed catalogue, while a sleet storm ticks against the window. Shall it be elephant garlic, Egyptian onions, the new hybrid squash called Kuta? Here's a new strain of edible Japanese chrysanthemums. The best light and steadiest warmth in the winter house surround the kitchen table. Readings and writings take place here. So do infrequent sewings and, properly protected with old newspapers, cleanings of harness and riding tack. And when the power fails, as it must three or four times a year, all repair to the kitchen table with the Family Lamp, readied against such emergencies with kerosene and neatly trimmed wick.

Where does the insomniac go? The mother or, increasingly, father, with baby at two a.m.? Indeed, not only does the dog lie down with the cat here, but in February enters the orphan lamb in an abused playpen. In March, a dozen new chicks. Once, briefly and by mistake, the wethered goat. Several times, peering mildly through the backdoor screen, the heifers. How disconcerting to raise up your eyes from the pie crust to find those large, sloe-eyed creatures looking in.

The morning kitchen is cheerful and workable, ready for the comfortable dishevelment of coffee brewing, bread slicing, the beating of eggs, the frying of bacon. It is a quiet time, good for elaborate planning of renovation, addition, improvement. The morning kitchen looks out on the rush-hour traffic at the bird feeder. The world is new again; the grosbeaks are back. The morning kitchen belongs to the idealist.

The man who cooks does so to best effect in a country kitchen. He is observed in his ritual of regenerating the sourdough starter after drawing off the two cups he needs for tomorrow's Sunday breakfast waffles. Indeed, every houseguest is a fresh excuse for his waffles with whipped butter and indigenous maple syrup. My favorite kitchen man is a cookstove artist with birch and poplar chunks in the maw of his Old Ironsides. Out of that oven he takes quick biscuits made tangy with Cheddar cheese shredded into the dough. He is also inventive with chutneys and sauces bearing the green tomato into the world.

Early in summer, color the country kitchen scarlet, a ripeness streaked with sunlight shading into purple. Rhubarb, the first lifeblood of the season, is ready early in June. Before the month is out, strawberries overtake it. Jam bubbles on the stove, pies drip in the oven. The kitchen becomes a factory of steam and smells, food mills, blanching vessels, tongs, jars, bottles, juices, and purées. It will turn out hundreds of pounds of produce between now and October. Everything surplus, everything homegrown or acquired at the local farmers' market marches into this command post to be dealt with, judiciously divided for present pleasure and future use.

In full summer, color the kitchen green, streaked with yellow. Erect as milkweed, asparagus pops above ground, thickens, and yields to the gatherer's knife. Early peas follow these spears into the freezer. Raspberries, plump and purpling, obedient to the calendar, come next. One blink of the eye and the bush beans, both yellow and green, are in. Mornings of stemming and blanching for the freezer. Half a sigh later, the Kentucky Wonders swarm up their tepees. The repetitive tasks are humbling. We all succumb to the benevolent tyranny of the garden as the first broccoli, the early cauliflower, a crowd of young lettuces overfill the kitchen, waiting to be sorted out. These to be consumed on the spot, those to be blanched and frozen, this to be canned, salted, pickled: all hands to the cutting board and colander.

Green and red and yellow, the summer kitchen is never empty. Cherries pop their pits. Beets bleed, undergoing purification. So alarming is the propensity of summer squash and zucchini to create a glut that entire cookbooks have been devoted to ingenious methods for disposing of them. Suddenly in mid-July the cucumbers arrive, slyly swelling under the protective mat of foliage.

The kitchen shifts into high gear. Bouquets of fresh dill shower the tabletop with yellow crumbs of blossom.. Basil, waiting to be buzzed into pesto in the blender, adds its lemony fragrance to an overall scent of vinegar and sugar, spices and earth smells. Peaches enter the marketplace. A bushel or two waits at the foot of the cellar stairs. Evenings, they rise, along with plums, to be halved and packed tight into jars. Two or three successive batches are covered with sugar syrup, submerged in the hot-water bath and boiled the allotted time. Next day, they adorn the winter shelves. Although the pears are still green on the tree, the red squirrels have found them, and the fruit must be picked and processed or all is lost. Blackcaps, arctic cloudberries, and cruelly brambled blackberries, diligently gathered day by day and frozen until a space can be cleared for them, wait to be sieved, sugared, and boiled into jam.

And then all attention is riveted on the corn patch. In spite of our having planted early, midseason, and late varieties, nature conspires to bring the entire crop in at once. For three glorious, hedonistic weeks we will dine on it nightly. We rush it from field to pot to table in under ten minutes and save the shucks for horses and heifers. Color the kitchen buttery yellow once the corn comes in. Any we can't eat on the spot is cut from the cob and sped into the freezer.

On hottest nights, color the kitchen crepuscular, only one light glowing, all harvest activities suspended. Consider those eight p.m. suppers with half a dozen fresh vegetables providing the main course. A generous salad based on three varieties of lettuce is overlaid with cukes, carrots, bits of broccoli, and icicles of raw kohlrabi, decorated with crumbs of feta cheese and buttered croutons. Hotter than ever tomorrow? Buzz the leftovers in the blender for cold lunchtime soup.

All too soon the first frost threatens. Gardens grow ghostly under their sheets and old drop cloths; forestalled for a week or two, Jack Frost returns. All over town the green tomatoes come indoors. In every kitchen arises the acrid tang of green-tomato pickle, chutney, chili; on every south-facing kitchen windowsill the most promising greenies line up to be coaxed ripe.

The ultimate reward, October, is celebrated with apples. Given the right degree of overlap, apples and green tomatoes will combine in the kitchen factory to create chutney. But apples alone account for pies and applesauce, cider and apple butter, cores, peels, and pomaces, enough to restore the country kitchen to its best level of frenzied disorder. Peelings for the animals, pomace for compost, quarts of applesauce set aside for winter.

Last, see the kitchen as history. In the all-important larder—in our case, shelves built into the capacious cellar entryway—stand jars full of fruits, pickles, jams, and jellies to stave off the megrims of those twenty-below-zero nights. Peanut-butter jars, still wearing the faint imprint on their lids of their sale prices, bespeak a kinder time, when the standard one-pound item sold for 69 cents. That same jar, now full of homemade strawberry, blackberry, plum, or grape jelly or jam, reads $1.19, $1.69, $2.09, $2.89! What's this? asks the archaeologist in the year 3000, $4.65? A dissertation in the year

3050, if the world lasts, will put forth hypotheses explaining the elevation of America's midday spread, this mash of the goober, to the expensive status of anchovy paste.

Here, too, stand old-fashioned Ball jars with wire bales and rubber-ring sealers for their glass lids. Although in the average kitchen these have been largely replaced by the far easier self-sealing metal lids, we are still gamely refilling our golden oldies. Many are inherited jars, handed down from grandmothers on both sides. Some have turned the delicate blue of antique glass and stand on a hanging shelf in the kitchen along with an excavated bottle whose raised letters proclaim SCOTTS EMULSION on one side, while on the other a fisherman carries a huge cod on his back. On the opposite wall a framed poster advertises the virtues of the Andes stove, a porcelain monster foursquare on its black bowlegs. *Makes poor cooks good and good cooks better,* reads the unabashed slogan.

Not an extravagant claim, its unvarnished declaration suits this country kitchen. Nothing fancy takes place here. Merely the steady rhythm of the life of the farm and the people who live here. Making all seasons better.

The Poet
and the Mule

The title of this essay is indeed "The Poet and the Mule."
Mule, despite all efforts on the part of alarmed proofreaders to
say otherwise, is not a misprint for *Muse.* The muse enters in,
as you might expect her to. Her part in the matter is a not
inconsiderable one. The connection between the poet and
this hardworking member of the equine family is of course
only a metaphorical one but it has little to do with stubbornness or even with singlemindedness, for neither poet nor mule
possesses these traits to a singular degree. The mule's problem is that she/he is a thinker, not an unquestioning per-
former. In the world of domesticated beasts of burden,
intelligence is not often an asset. The poet's difficulty, too, is
that she/he thinks and beyond thinking, feels; and beyond feeling, verbalizes whatever is leaping the synapses in an attempt
to speak to this universal but frequently unrecognized process
in his or her fellow creatures.

The mule is not noted for its physical beauty. It does

not have the grace of limb, the fluidity of motion that the horse possesses. Frequently the mule, especially the larger, heavy-duty or draft mule, is an ungainly-looking animal, something like Delmore Schwartz's heavy bear, "the central ton of every place." A shuffler, perhaps, but surefooted, safest of all descenders to the bottom of the Grand Canyon, for example, nimblest of all workers in the narrow tobacco rows, the emerging cotton crop, and now prized in the tree nursery for that same skill. A specialist, you might say, much as you might say of the poet, who specializes in compression, density, the narrow confines of the line, its metrics, its verbal tricks at the ends of rows. The funny-looking poet, the fop of the TV situation comedy, the person of pithy words.

Hybrids, both of them, endurers, lasting beyond any demographic prediction, poet and mule. How much has been said of the former, how little of the latter! The poet confesses an inordinate fondness for the species, and a longstanding curiosity about its history, especially its place in the history of the United States. It is a story that has not, the poet thinks, yet been told.

William Faulkner has put his imprimatur on the subject, exhorting the poet, in his novel *Sartoris,* thusly: "Some Homer of the cotton fields should sing the saga of the mule and of his place in the South." Faulkner, alas, is also responsible for perpetuating some of the myths about the mule's intractable disposition, of which more later.

Some people do not know what makes a mule. It is the hybrid offspring of a horse and an ass. Ambrose Bierce, in 1881, wrote the following quatrain:

> *"Hail, holy Ass!" the quiring angels sing;*
> *"Priest of Unreason, and of Discords King!*

Great co-Creator, let Thy glory shine:
God made all else; the Mule, the Mule is thine!" *

(The term donkey has crept into our language as a polite substitute for the word ass and now appears frequently as its
synonym. In actual fact, the two animals differ only in stature, the donkey being a smaller version of the ass.) More
particularly, the mule is the result of standing a female horse,
called a mare, to the male ass, called a jack. The other cross,
the result of breeding the female ass, known as a jenny, to the
male horse or stallion, although physiologically possible, is less
commonly utilized. The resultant foal will be smaller, having
developed in the uterus of the smaller dam, or mother, than
the foal from the mare-and-jack breeding. The term for the
jenny-stallion cross is *hinny.* Hinnies are prized by their few
owners as the more horselike hybrid and are said to be popular
for light work in Ireland, Spain, and South America.

Both male mules and male hinnies are sterile. Nature
will not cross this barrier twice, it seems, in this direction.
Female mules can and do conceive, or settle, to use the appropriate term, but seldom bear live foals. Spontaneous abortion
is common in these cases. Indeed, so rare is the circumstance
of a live birth that Theodore Savory, writing in *Scientific American,* cites a Latin idiom, *cum mula peperit,* "when a mule foals,"
as an ancient parallel to the idiom "once in a blue moon." The
only documented accounts of live foals born to molly mules in
the United States date back to 1920 at Texas A&M College.

The gene that makes the poet does not seem to be trans-
missible, either. Generations of M.D.s and lawyers are com-

---

*Ambrose Bierce, "The Devil's Dictionary," *The Collected Writings of Ambrose Bierce*
(Plainview, N.Y.: Books for Libraries Press, 1946), p. 199.

monplace. *Cum mula peperit,* do poet offspring succeed their parents.

At any rate, when, once in a blue moon, a molly or mare mule foals, the birth will occur at the end of a 10½-month period of gestation. The length of gestation in horses is eleven months, in asses, ten; how tidy, how orderly, thinks the poet, that the rare mixed birth should fall precisely between the two. How like a metrical fact of life; as for example, when a hexameter line breaks naturally with a caesura after the first three feet. But that is putting the hendecasyllabics before the mule, as it were. The point I wanted to make was that whatever our subject, we need to devise a special language to investigate it. You can see how the language of mules and horses resembles the language of prosody, with its iambs and enjambements, its couplets and synecdoches. For here we have hinny and jenny, jack and molly, standing and settling, dropping and foaling, dams and sires. We have not yet even spoken of withers and fetlocks, chestnuts, stifles, frogs, polls, pasterns, croups, cannons, barrels and hocks. But it is clear that we need jargon, the technical terminology or characteristic idiom of specialists in a particular activity, if we are to go beyond the Dick-and-Jane stage of communicating information or suppositions about a chosen topic. The poets have greatly simplified their technical jargon in the twentieth century, perhaps despairing of an educated readership in an era of vocational rather than classical education. For better or worse, the poets speak less frequently of epistemological frameworks and semiotic patterns than formerly. Still, as T. S. Eliot has it, "If you complain that a poet is obscure, and apparently ignoring you, the reader, or that he is speaking only to a limited circle of initiates from which you are excluded—remember that what he may have been trying to do, was to put something in words which could not be said in any other way, and therefore in a language which may be worth the trouble of learning."* The same principle may apply with equal hauteur to any area of expertise.

Swifter than oxen, sturdier than horses, the mule is the oldest hybrid developed by humankind and undoubtedly the most useful economically. Geneticists would also claim it is biologically the most interesting. Indeed, the literature is peppered with chromosome charts. The mule is mentioned in the Bible, appears frequently in Homer, flourished as a draft animal across the Peloponnesus, is praised by Marco Polo, who met a vigorous strain of mules in central Asia, and was widely used across southern Europe before the Renaissance. The mule was bred to work in the fields, to draw wagons and carts, to be ridden under saddle, and even to race. The mule is a tougher animal than the horse. It can endure more hardship, stay in better condition under adversity and hard labor. The mule is more careful than the horse; not as likely to blemish itself. By and large the mule is longer-lived. A mule will not overeat and founder as the horse, let loose in the grain bin, can be counted on to do. The mule does not overheat as readily as the horse. Although perhaps more susceptible to respiratory ailments, it has a physiologic ability to withstand greater degrees of dehydration than the horse.† Thus you might say that the mule can put up with more ignorance and mismanagement on the part of the teamster than the horse.

Specific sizes and shapes of mules were bred in certain areas. In Poitou, a former province known as the granary of France, draft-type jacks with extraordinarily heavy coats were

*T. S. Eliot, *On Poetry and Poets* (New York: Farrar, Straus & Giroux, 1957), pp. 111–112.

†Conversation with Tex Taylor, D.V.M., Texas A&M University, April 16, 1980.

bred to mares each year as early in recorded history as the eleventh century and their mule offspring were raised and trained to pull singly or in teams. In 1866, fifty thousand mares were bred to Poitou jacks alone and "the yearly export of young mules amounted to between two and three million dollars."* What that would amount to in present-day dollars boggles the mind.

Italy, Spain, and Malta also developed as breeding centers in the eighteenth century. The mule was not generally accepted as a work animal in Great Britain, however, till the latter years of the eighteenth century. Its adoption by the British exactly parallels the expansion of the British empire, and would all by itself provide, the poet thinks, a pithy subject for a history dissertation. The mule came to be much prized for service in the army in India and other British outposts. Indeed, difficult conquest and mule came to be synonymous in the imagination of explorers. Mules followed the miners to and from gold deposits in the Klondike. Mules crossed the Isthmus of Panama on the world's most-used pack trail. Twenty-mule teams dragged wagons loaded with borax with a total weight in excess of seventy-three thousand pounds across Death Valley. And mules were used in our own colonial adventures, notably in Mexico and the Philippines.

In 1945, nine hundred American artillery mules were marched 750 miles from upper Burma, where they had served honorably during the campaign to liberate that country from the Japanese, across the Hump, as the Himalayas were known, into China. They were to be delivered to irregular Chinese Nationalists in their guerrilla war against the Chinese Communists. A fascinating account of this journey was published

*L. W. Knight, M.D., *The Breeding and Rearing of Jacks, Jennets and Mules* (Nashville, Tenn.: The Cumberland Press, 1902), p. 108.

by John Rand in *The New Yorker* magazine some years later. Rand was not a mule skinner by profession, merely an effete Eastern horseman. His view of the nature of the mule is particularly interesting for its dispassion. In the following passage I would ask that you construct a running analogy between mule and poet. A metaphor elaborated in this fashion is called a conceit.

> Mules have their own personalities, but, like soldiers, they fall into several broad types. Some of ours, like some soldiers, went about their work without any fuss; they stood quietly while they were being loaded, and marched quietly all day. Others were forever kicking and bucking and getting out of line. And still others kept formation but constantly nipped at and otherwise pestered the mules in front of them. . . . Like most people who are used to horses, I had a prejudice against mules when I joined the pack artillery, but in the tough Burma going I quickly got over it. Mules may not be built for speed, but they can do prodigious things. I have seen them climb rocks that I couldn't negotiate on all fours. I have seen them topple into gorges and disappear far below, turning over and over, a tangle of legs, ears, and load, and later, at the bottom, I have found some of them on their feet, placidly grazing. (Not all of them, needless to say; I have found some with their necks or backs broken.)*

To examine the conceit backwards: not all poets survive the circumstances of their downfall. Indeed, a considerable cult has grown up around the famous poet suicides. A Berryman, a Hart Crane, a Plath, or a Sexton excites the combined prurience and sympathetic imagination of the general

*John A. Rand, "900 Mules," *The New Yorker*, November 27, 1954, p. 158.

public to an astonishing pitch. Actuarial tables indicate that psychiatrists, dentists, painters, and lawyers all have higher suicide rates than poets, but none of these groups captures the interest of the general readership. Is it because the public expects the poet, that maverick, to be tougher than the rest of the community? Not subject to the same emotional stresses? Not requiring the same rations, as it were, in order to keep working?

The prodigiousness of the poet has been frequently remarked and needs no documentation here. As for nipping and pestering their own kind, perhaps poets are no better or worse than politicians or other performing artists. It is a trait that has been deplored, or admired, depending on circumstances, and frequently receives more attention than the poetry itself. Famous poet antipathies spring to mind—William Carlos Williams and T. S. Eliot, Louise Bogan and Muriel Rukeyser, Yvor Winters and Robinson Jeffers. We have Allen Tate, writing from his perch as Consultant in Poetry to the Library of Congress in 1944 that Edna St. Vincent Millay is "definitely, from first to last, a minor lyricist, and in my opinion never the equal from any point of view of . . . Miss Moore and several other women poets of our time." And Allen Tate on Amy Lowell: "I find Miss Lowell interesting from the historical point of view only; she seems more remote than Mrs. Browning, and not quite so good (which isn't very good)."*

Some poets, to be sure, go about their work without any fuss. Most poets, like most mules, die unsung. The mythology of each species persists.

Alas, the Rand China-Burma story has a sad ending. When surra, a tropical blood disease, was discovered in several of the

*Allen Tate, *Sixty American Poets 1896–1944* (Washington, D.C.: Library of Congress, 1954), pp. 71, 85.

mules, orders were given to destroy them all. There were no bulldozers available to prepare mass graves for several hundred animals, but Rand resourcefully located some deep gullies, into which the mules could be pushed once they were shot. The Corps of Engineers then dynamited the gully walls around them in order to bury the corpses. Again, I quote: "I don't know what the Chinese made of this. They may have thought that we barbarians were offering a mammoth sacrifice to celebrate the end of the war. At any rate, they didn't go along with it. As soon as the dirt stopped falling, peasants went to work digging the mules out so they could eat the meat."

Naive, wrongheaded, wasteful, and finally cruel, the army prevailed. The mule epic ends with the death of the troop in a strange land, bearing, as Rand concludes, "the obscure distinction of being the farthest ranging, and perhaps the last, world travelers of their species."

The exiled poet has the advantage in such situations:

If I should die think only this of me
that there's some corner of a foreign field that is forever England
or:

If I forget thee, o Jerusalem
may my right hand forget its cunning.

But the poet has overturned the chronology of the story. This lengthy digression began with the statement that the usefulness of the mule came rather late to Great Britain and was not fully established there until the latter part of the 1700s.

Not unexpectedly, then, the notion of breeding mules crossed the ocean with the colonists. Agriculture was to be the primary activity in the new settlements; livestock formed a vital link in the food chain. Foundation animals for American breeds had of course to be imported from European countries and from Great Britain. The voyages were costly, dangerous and chancy. There exists a whole body of literature exploring the then best-known ways to secure horses, asses, cattle and other livestock for transport, up to and including pamphlets published by the U.S. Army in World War II on moving mules by barge.

Although some few mules had already made their way into Louisiana by way of trade with the Spaniards in New Mexico, George Washington was the first voice heard in the New World in praise of this hybrid, and he is responsible for introducing the first breeding program in the New World, at Mount Vernon. Quite obviously his eminence lent an aura of prestige to what appeared at first a purely quixotic venture. Upon learning of Washington's interest in raising mules, Florida Blanca, the Spanish minister of state, prevailed upon King Charles III to relax the royal edict forbidding the exportation of breeding jacks, and in December of 1785 Charles's gift to Washington arrived. One of the two jacks he sent had died en route, but two jennies and one sturdy four-year-old jack arrived in reasonable condition. Washington named the young jack Royal Gift and stood him at stud that very season. In fact, a rather delightful advertisement for his prowess appeared at the end of February in a Philadelphia paper. Although signed by John Fairfax, his overseer, the language may well be Washington's.

> ROYAL GIFT—A jack Ass of the first place in the kingdom of Spain will cover mares and jennies (the asses) at Mount Vernon the ensuing spring. The first for ten, the latter for fifteen pounds in the season. Royal Gift is four years old, is between 14- 1 half and 15 hands

high and will grow, it is said, till he is twenty- or twenty-
five years of age. He is very bony and stout made, of
dark color, with light belly and legs. The advantages,
which are many, to be derived from the propagation of
asses from this animal, the first of the kind that ever
was in North America, and the usefulness of mules bred
from a Jack of his size, either for the road or team, are
well known to those who are acquainted with this mon-
grel race. For the information of those who are not, it
may be enough to add, that their great strength, longev-
ity, hardiness, and cheap support, give them a prefer-
ence of horses that is scarcely to be imagined. . . .*

The stud fee for breeding a jack to mares was always
smaller than to its own kind, the jenny, and this discrepancy
in fee remains common practice to this day.

A hand is a primitive but persistent unit of measure in
equine jargon; it equals four inches. Height is measured in a
straight line from the top of the withers—the highest point of
the shoulder—to the ground. Of course the statement about
the jack's continuing growth is nonsense; the equine reaches
full growth at age four or five.

For the next hundred years, it is interesting to note, virtually every advertisement for breeding jacks referred to the
fact that the particular animal was "very bony and stout made,"
and all over Kentucky and Tennessee and Missouri these con-
formational traits were taken to be virtues. The canard that
a mule needs less to eat than a horse also meant that stingy
rations were offered these denizens of the cotton fields and
coal mines for the next hundred years. In actual fact, the

---

*Cited in Robert Byron Lamb, *The Mule in Southern Agriculture* (Berkeley: University of California Press, 1963), p. 6. I should like to acknowledge my special in-
debtedness to Lamb, whose monograph motivated me to undertake this essay.

working mule requires pound for pound the same calories as the draft horse. In practice, many an unthrifty malnourished animal was sent out to plow, in consort with the unthrifty malnourished tenant farmer, sharecropper or slave.

And how often since the end of the era of patronage has it been suggested that the true poet can survive on reduced rations for the sake of his/her art? Thoreau, on hearing that a certain East India merchant had gone out to the empire to make his fortune before undertaking the writing of poetry, remarked with an asperity unbecoming in one of New England's wiliest freeloaders: "He should have gone up garret at once."*

And Paul Theroux, in a lecture delivered at the Library of Congress for which he was paid out of the Library's patronage purse known as the Whittall Fund, focused his attack on patronage extended to writers in the colleges and universities' creative writing departments "in whose precincts we find the writer-in-residence, the visiting writer, the professor who writes when the spirit moves him, and the scribbling students." All of these aspirants, suggests Theroux, would be better served by a reduction in funding. This would mean "a richer literary life, and perhaps signal the return of the man of letters. [No mention of the woman.] Art is not such a frail thing as it has often been made out to be, or so badly in need of moneyed well-wishers."

Thus once again we are counseled that it is good for the poet to go hungry; the poet, like the mule, is sturdy enough to get by in reduced circumstances.

In the same year that he received Royal Gift, Washington acquired two jennies, and a jack from the island of Malta, a

---

*Henry David Thoreau, *Walden: A Writer's Edition*, Holt, Rinehart & Winston, 1961, p. 42.

shipment arranged for him by the Marquis de Lafayette. The Maltese stock were smaller in stature, finer-boned and rather more gracefully proportioned than the Spanish strain. Because the soil is thin and the grazing marginal on this island, it was conjectured by the early American breeders that these animals had been stunted by their environment and would do rather better on the pasturage of the American South. Time bore them out; the Maltese bloodlines came to be highly prized for their refinement in succeeding generations.

Washington's plan, as he elucidated upon it in a letter to Arthur Young, was to breed the Spanish jack for

> heavy slowdraught; and the others for the saddle or lighter carriages. From these, altogether, I hope to secure a race of extraordinary goodness, which will stock the country. Their longevity and cheap keeping will be circumstances much in their favor. I am convinced, from the little experiments I have made with the ordinary mules (which perform as much labor, with vastly less feeding than horses), that those of a superior quality will be the best cattle we can employ for the harness; and indeed in a few years, I intend to drive no other in my carriage, having appropriated for the sole purpose of breeding them, upwards of twenty of my best mares.*

After a little more reflection, Washington crossed the jenny progeny of his Maltese sire and Royal Gift. The young stud he obtained he named Compound, a jack combining the best traits of the two lines. Compound serviced Washington's twenty coach mares, by all accounts creating a strain of superior mules. This breeding success inspired other farmers throughout the Tidewater to emulate the first President's example. Clearly,

*John C. Fitzpatrick, ed., *The Diaries of George Washington 1748–1799*, vol. 3 (Boston and New York: Houghton Mifflin Company, 1925), p. 138.

Washington was the father of his country in more than one sense, for the working mule made all else possible in the Southern agricultural economy.

Jefferson, too, became a mule enthusiast, although he imported no stock, relying instead on local animals and particularly on good-size mules brought in from Kentucky. Alas, Jefferson perpetuated the notion that mules require less fodder than horses, and boasted that his big mules kept fit on only a little more than half the corn ration allotted his horses.*

Henry Clay, also a mule fancier, imported several Spanish jacks for his stud.†

Early in the 1800s the bluegrass basin of Kentucky became a favorable breeding ground. The same grassy savannahs over limestone that fortify the present-day Thoroughbred racehorse industry cherished the mule nurseries of the nineteenth century. The mule business enlarged itself mightily in Kentucky and spread to the Nashville basin of Tennessee, which also proved a favorable milieu for the raising of mules on its phosphatic limestone pastures of bluegrass and clover.

In Missouri, which developed a parallel mule nursery in the 1820s, it was the practice to use large draft mares for breeding stock. This led to the development of the famous hefty Missouri mule. But it is worth noting that the American farm horse was a pony-size creature for the most part well into the nineteenth century. Washington's meticulous records year by year in his diaries list the heights, colors, and ages of his horses, and almost all of his stock fall within the 13½- to 14½-hand range. Only with the importation of Percheron

---

*Morris Betts, ed., *Thomas Jefferson's Farm Book* (Princeton: Princeton University Press, 1953), p. 138.

†More about Henry Clay's breeding stock can be found in Frank C. Mills, *History of American Jacks & Mules* (Hutchinson, Kan.: Hutch-Line, 1971), pp. 14–15 ff.

stock from France did the size of the farm horse begin to change.

By the time of World War I, this hybrid had invaded every hamlet, every plantation, every family farm. We might call this period of acceptance of the mule at all levels in working society the *Palgrave's Golden Treasury,* or *Best-Loved Poems of the American People* era. It was the golden age of the agrarian mule, an age we might loosely equate with the narrative poems of Longfellow, Whittier, James Whitcomb Riley, an age of genre poems with mass appeal that, like the mule, grew by geometric progression into the early portion of the twentieth century. In this connection, the poet William Meredith shared with me a quotation from the jacket blurb of Robert Frost's *Mountain Interval,* first published in 1916. The anonymous blurb writer has written: "Mr. Frost captures the New England experience better than any living poet—except Miss Wilkins." Alas, who was Miss Wilkins? She is as forgotten today as Imported Mammoth, "the greatest jack sire of all"* or the "tra-landage [from 'tra la la'] song of the hostler which is used for the sole purpose of exciting the amativeness of the jack."†

Throughout the nineteenth century, mules found their way as draft and pack animals in the army, into the westward trade, even on the sugar plantations of the West Indies, but their chief use was in the Lower South on cotton plantations and croplands. It became established practice to breed and raise mules in the bluegrass basin, then ship them into cotton country.

Southern grasslands could not compete with the lush grazings of the bluegrass and prairie-grass basins. In summer the orchard grasses crisped and burned, making year-round

*Mills, p. 64.
†Ibid., p. 62.

maintenance of young stock a difficult undertaking. But another less tangible factor also entered into the reluctance of
southern farmers to establish breeding operations. The high-
density mule areas were also the high-density slave areas. All
the frustration and outrage of the black man, slave or, later,
tenant or sharecropper, was visited on the animal he ruled:
". . . the work stock suffered under the care of croppers,
tenants or wagehands," one writer suggests.* Frederick Law
Olmsted in the early 1850s observed that ". . . horses cannot
bear the treatment that they always must get from negroes . . .
while mules will bear cudgelling, and lose a meal or two now
and then, and not be materially injured.† Indeed, the only
creature more lowly than the slave or tenant farmer in the
cotton economy was the poor benighted mule. At the bottom
of the order, the mule endured privation and abuse and was
widely believed to deserve this treatment for its sheer cussed-
ness.

To the underbeast of the equine world are variously as-
cribed stubbornness, deceit, and a wicked temperament. Although its intelligence, courage, and acuity of vision and hearing
are attested to by knowledgeable partisans of the mule world,
as little is heard of these virtues as is heard of the great mass
of poets who go humbly about the accretion of poems without
wild gestures, drunken displays of temper, or public orgies.

Despite the fact that the average citizen has never per-
sonally encountered one, the question of the mule's disposition
has for the popular imagination the same sort of fascination
Anthony Hecht speaks of when he writes, in *The New York
Times Book Review*: ". . . the public has come to expect poets
to be weird, scandalous and unpleasant, and society has con-

*Lamb, p. 27.
†Ibid.

[115]

trived to arrange things to make it easy for them to be so.
. . . If poets provoke any interest whatever on the part of
the general public, that interest is not in the poetry *per se* but
in the poets' lives, which are widely held . . . to be highly
peculiar and unsavory."*

How odd it is that the poet, albeit unread, figures so
large in the popular imagination. (Perhaps this inflated afflatus
is one of our problems—we are scapegoat and oracle all in
one.)

How little the mule figures in American letters, even at
the level of folktale, is remarkable, considering its actual socio-
political role. Only William Faulkner pays the mule any significant notice. In his rollicking horserace novel, *The Reivers,*
Faulkner indulges in the following disquisition:

> A mule which will gallop for a half-mile in the single
> direction elected by its rider even one time becomes a
> neighborhood legend; one that will do it consistently time
> after time is an incredible phenomenon. Because, unlike
> a horse, a mule is far too intelligent to break its heart
> for glory running around the rim of a mile-long saucer.
> In fact, I rate mules second only to rats in intelli-
> gence. . . .
> The rat of course I rate first. He lives in your house
> without helping you to buy it or build it or repair it or
> keep the taxes paid; he eats what you eat without help-
> ing you raise it or buy it or even haul it into the
> house. . . .
> The mule I rate second. But second only because
> you can make him work for you. But that too only
> within his own rigid self-set regulations. He will not
> permit himself to eat too much. He will draw a wagon

*Anthony Hecht, in *The New York Times Book Review,* February 27, 1982, p. 3.

or a plow, but he will not run a race. He will not try to jump anything he does not indubitably know beforehand he can jump; he will not enter any place unless he knows of his own knowledge what is on the other side; he will work for you patiently for ten years for the chance to kick you once. In a word, free of the obligations of ancestry and the responsibilities of posterity, he has conquered not only life but death too and hence is immortal; were he to vanish from the earth today, the same chanceful biological combination which produced him yesterday would produce him a thousand years hence, unaltered, unchanged, incorrigible still within the limitations which he himself had proved and tested; still free, still coping. . . .*

The kicking canard, like the myth about the mule's reduced nutritional needs, thus received further reinforcement from Faulkner. A mule that has been systematically maltreated for ten years may very well await a chance to get even. A mule that has been treated equably will entertain no more rebellious notions than the average well-raised horse or pony.

Nor is it true that the mule will not race. Today's handsome Thoroughbred mules are running as fleetly as horses on tracks throughout the Southwest. In endurance races over distances as great as one hundred miles, to be traversed in less than twenty-four hours, the well-bred conditioned mule is regularly in the ribbons, in the East as well as in the West.

The mules kept pace with the one-crop feudal system of agriculture that gripped Southern agrarian practices throughout the nineteenth and well into the twentieth century. Although of course the Civil War caused huge losses in all kinds of livestock, the mule fared least badly. Horses were lost in

*William Faulkner, *The Reivers* (New York: Random House, 1962), p. 121–122.

[117]

cavalry battles and not replaced; oxen were eaten as times grew increasingly hard. A cultural prejudice against eating the flesh of jackasses seems to have saved the breeding stock. Although the South had fewer mules in 1870 than before the Civil War, the ensuing decade saw their numbers swell. By the last decade of the nineteenth century, the use of mules had reached westward into Texas and Oklahoma, as cotton acreage increased in these regions. Since most of these farmers were migrants from the Lower South, they were already culturally predisposed to plow with mules. By 1900, 2½ million mules trod the southern farmlands of this nation. Along inland waterways mules muscled barges laden with flour, timber and coal. One of the most famous of these mule routes, the 184-mile Chesapeake & Ohio Canal, which ran from Washington, D.C., to Cumberland, Maryland, was a major supply line. By 1875 the C&O Canal, each of its 540 barges tugged along by two mules, working in tandem in six-hour shifts, moved almost a million tons of cargo each day.

Despite a drop in the number and size of mule-breeding farms with the onset of World War I, the peak of the curve of mule population was not reached until 1925, when the number of mules in the South alone reached 4½ million and stood at six million nationwide. The army mule continued to play an important role well into the twentieth century. More than five thousand mules were killed in action in World War II. Mules served up to the Korean War; the last thirty-one army mules were mustered out of service in 1957.

In truth, the mule was everywhere by 1925, serving not only the cotton holdings of the South, but the sugarcane plantations and rice fields of Louisiana, the tobacco lands of the Carolinas, the wheat, barley, corn and other grain acreages of the middle and upper West, the truck gardens of Virginia's

Eastern Shore, even the forests of upper New York State. Technology, of course, displaced this hybrid little by little. The coming of the boll weevil also sharply reduced cotton acreage in Georgia, Alabama and South Carolina.

The Depression of the thirties further tended to reduce cotton acreage and emphasized for the first time the importance in the South of raising feed crops for livestock and food crops for humans. But it was the tractor that finally spelled doom to the mule industry. Little by little, year by year, the mule gave way to the machine.

The most moving account of this technological displacement of men and mules is to be found in a study done by Betty Carter, former publisher of the Greenville, Mississippi, *Delta Democrat-Times.* After eloquently detailing the worklife and symbiotic relationship between mule and tenant for over a hundred years in the eighteen counties of Mississippi comprising the Delta, she concludes with an account of how suddenly the old system capitulated between 1940 and 1950. "Dogfood factories rounded up the mules of entire plantations, buying for two cents a pound animals that had been purchased for a hundred dollars apiece. The Delta and Pine Land Plantation, one of the largest, made its final decision so suddenly that in 1948 it sold a hundred two-year-old mules that had not yet even been broken."*

According to all demographic predictions, the mule should have become extinct in the United States by 1960. Somehow, humbly and haphazardly, it hung on. In the sophisticated nuclear age of the eighties, the mule persists. It is estimated that approximately 250,000 mules now flourish across the contiguous forty-eight states, the majority of them concentrated

*American Heritage, vol. 28 (December 1976), p. 63.

in the Southwestern tier.* Now largely a sporting animal, today's mule is enjoying a considerable renaissance in Texas. Robert Cantwell, a writer for *Sports Illustrated,* reports that "about 1,000 glossy, well-fed mules live around Bishop," Texas where "last spring [1976], 40,000 people lined the streets . . . to watch the parade that opened the annual Mule Days Celebration."

A Swiss veterinarian and a native Texan clinician, working closely together for the last several years at Texas A&M in a breeding program to rescue the American jack and mule stock, speak enthusiastically about the virtues of the hybrid. Both men see a future for the "new" streamlined Thoroughbred mule as a sporting animal and predict a resurgence of its use, in a sturdier variety, as a draft and work animal. By utilizing our finest jacks, Dr. Taylor feels that we can and will be of immense use in the Third World to upgrade their stock. "No more of this any-size-which-shape mule for the plow," he says. Through selective breeding, the mule can be tailored to special needs.

In the South, mules are again in demand for small acreage allotments, for example, in tobacco, where farmers find it financially impractical to fuel a tractor. In the Northeast, draft mules are in vogue for selective cutting of timber stands. Whatever a good "twitching" horse can do, literally twitching a single felled tree trunk across the debris of the forest floor to a staging area, a well-broken mule can do even more stolidly and sensibly.

In an era gaudy with television specials, multi-cinemas, huge sporting events and popular musicians, the poet, like the mule, has endured. A renaissance—and it is not a quiet one—is in process. There are 3,536 publishing poets in the United

---

*Conversation with Dr. Paul Hutchins, President, American Donkey and Mule Society, Denton, Texas, April 1982.

States, according to Poets & Writers' directory. The *American Poetry Review* has 25,000 subscribers. There are those, like Terrence Des Pres, who declare that the state of the art "is not splendid. . . . The main drift of our poetry in the last few years has been deplorable for its thinness of vision, its lack of amplitude and will."* There are those who call for cross-fertilization between art and science, as does biologist Lewis Thomas, most eloquently decrying the fact that "physics professors, most of them, look with revulsion on assignments to teach their subject to poets."† Thomas chides his fellow scientists; the poets, out of all humankind, he feels, desperately need this exposure to how things stand in the various branches of science.

In 1968, the late Archibald MacLeish daringly predicted, "Far from being an extinguished form of decorative writing that is going out of use, poetry is going to become an increasingly vital part of contemporary life."‡

We cannot look to either of these hybrids, poet or mule, to save the world. But we can perhaps take comfort from the knowledge that each of them endures. The thought of this little mule-blip, like the poet-blip, lightens the heart these sad days.

*Terrence Des Pres, in *The Nation,* May 2, 1981, pp. 521–522.
†Lewis Thomas, in *The New York Times Magazine,* March 14, 1982, p. 9.
‡*The New York Times,* April 22, 1982.

WINTER

Scotch Highlanders

The first time I saw a mass of Scotch Highland cattle in motion, the herd was coming down to its shelter in late afternoon. There they were rewarded with a sprinkling of feed in the trough, as an inducement to arrive regularly at this hour. Thus, new calves trotting behind their mothers could be counted, and note taken of the general state of the animals.

I was struck by the sheer heft of the cattle, a moving carpet of chestnut matting surging home, gradually differentiating into cows and bulls, calves and yearlings. We walked among them with impunity, patting this one and that, noting that the herd's two sires were as unruffled and gentle as the cows. And before you could say American Scotch Highland Breeders' Association, Knoll Farm Samantha—a red heifer born on Bastille Day—became ours. To keep her company we acquired another yearling red heifer, Hopscotch Hope, who is one-quarter Jersey. In a year they have gained several hundred pounds between them, grown long-backed and sturdy, and enlarged the merest buds of horns into formidable, almost-full sets.

"Scotch cows will do upon the poorest pasture," wrote the Englishman Thomas Hale in 1758, "and they will suit some who cannot rise to the price of other kinds." Today, however, the Highlander is a chic item and fetches chic prices. Newly weaned bull calves in the summer of 1981 went for $500 apiece, rather better than market prices for other breeds. Registered, bred cows sold for $1,300 or more. Highland bulls, however, don't fetch comparably high prices simply because sizable herds for them to service do not exist. Most cross-breeding programs utilize Highland cows and, say, Hereford or Longhorn bulls, which further limits the need for the purebred Highland sire.

Because of the insulating qualities of the Highlander's hide and hair, Highland meat lacks the thick outer layer of fat common to many other breeds. The fat is evenly dispersed throughout the flesh, giving it an excellent marble. Fine-grained and tender, Highland beef graces the table of the Queen of England, who maintains a herd at Balmoral Castle and makes a practice of flying this beef in for her own meals when she travels outside her island.

Before there were Black Angus, before polled Herefords or Shorthorns or Santa Gertrudis were known, tough little Scotch Highland cattle roamed the hilly regions and west coastal islands of Scotland, subsisting on brush and browse. Their written records go back to the twelfth century. Archaeological evidence places them there as early as the sixth. The characteristics of the breed have remained remarkably uniform since that time. Hardy, quiet, docile and long-lived are the easily substantiated claims put forth to extol these wonderfully prehistoric-looking creatures. With their fearsome horns and mucilaginous muzzles they suggest in the aggregate a herd of returned mastodons.

The Highlander's small body size means that it requires

relatively little feed. A thrifty forager, it maintains weight gain in situations where more massive breeds cannot thrive. No other cattle subsist on less inviting browse. On the Stroh ranch in southern Colorado, described as typical arroyo terrain of sagebrush and piñon trees, the shaggy Highlanders fend for themselves year-round without so much as a calving shed for shelter. They are fed hay only during blizzard conditions and finish out on grass rather than grain. Deep, long-bodied, low-set, the Highlander is profusely haired with a double coat. The undercoat is soft and downy, providing superior insulation. The long outercoat, which may grow to thirteen inches, is well oiled to shed rain and snow. Tests conducted in Canada to assess the cold-weather vigor of various breeds reflect this built-in insulation. The Highland breed proved hardier than any available bovine tested except the bison.

Eye problems are almost unknown in the breed. The exceptionally long forelock hangs down over the eyes and provides excellent protection against blackflies, deerflies, face flies, and bot flies, all of which bedevil other livestock in the Northeast. To mosquitoes and no-see-ums the Highlander presents an impervious surface.

Highland cows make excellent mothers. Because of the breed's short neck and small head, calving problems are rare. Cows do not hide out their newborn, but stay with them until they are old enough to travel. Newborn calves do not chill, even when born in severe weather. Dwarfism is virtually unknown. Losses are modest; diseases seldom strike.

Moreover, the Highlander is famous for its homing instinct. If one strays through a fence or becomes separated from the herd during a blizzard, it will almost invariably find its way back to the fold. In the West heroic tales are told of Highland cattle homing through snow, fogs and deep drifts to their own territory. Our two heifers have wandered into the woods, ambled onto a dirt road a mile from home, trudged along it to our mailbox, and escorted themselves almost half a mile uphill to their pasture gate.

But perhaps the signal virtue and key to future growth of the breed is its hybrid vigor, or *heterosis,* to use the geneticist's term. Because the Highlander descends unchanged from a genetically uniform population and is thus of a different genotype from other cattle, it provides a successful cross with Herefords, Shorthorns, Longhorns and Brahmas, to name the most popular combinations.

"They dress out like a rabbit," warned the local pundit, who had come to deliver a truckload of fence posts and stayed half the morning to inspect Samantha and Hope. Official statistics, however, prove him wrong. Over the last eighteen years Scotch Highland cattle have received thirteen grand championships or reserve championships with purebred and crossbred animals. In Colorado, the Stroh Ranch Highland-Shorthorn crosses consistently win the Western Livestock Show in Denver. Last year's winning heifer, which took top honors for quality and yield of carcass, weighed in at 619 pounds. To get technical about it, the fat thickness was .38 inch, the ribeye area 13.38, the carcass index 52.22. Translated, that means that the layer of fat measured over the animal's twelfth rib was only 38/100-inch thick. The ribeye area, site of rib steaks, measured 13.38 square inches. Of this 619-pound carcass— boned out and trimmed closely and uniformly—52.22 percent was returned in the four retail cuts established by USDA standards, namely, round, loin, rib, and chuck. These are hardly rabbitlike figures.

Although forty states are represented in the current American Scotch Highland Breeders' Association (ASHBA: P.O.

Box 5747, Lafayette, Indiana 47903) membership list, ranging from two farms in Rhode Island to fifty in the state of Washington, the three main pockets of breeders are in Colorado, Minnesota and the north-central states, and northern New England. Maine, New Hampshire, Vermont and Massachusetts account for thirty-eight farms. More than 13,000 registrations were recorded nationwide in 1977. Numerous unregistered others, like our part-Jersey heifer, graze across the continent.

Virtually all herds live outdoors all winter and are fed supplemental hay only when the snow gets too deep for any grazing. Many breeders report that when the snow crust is thick, Highlanders will break it with their horns and paw down through substantial snowfalls to suitable browse. On a thirty-five-below-zero night last January, in the teeth of a forty-mile-per-hour wind out of the north, Samantha and Hope abandoned the stuffy confines of their shed in favor of bedding down in the air-conditioned pine grove. Is it ever too cold for the Highland breed? In Minnesota one breeder advertises his "unpampered cattle, raised out of doors in a climate less than ideal" where temperatures plummet to fifty below.

Crossbreeding with Longhorns, Shorthorns, Herefords and Brahmas tends to produce rugged cattle, popular on Western ranches where livestock must forage over considerable distances and travel miles between watering places, munching contentedly on undesirable weeds, brush, and tree leaves. Daniel Flynn, on Wilbraham Mountain in Massachusetts, began seven years ago with three Highland heifers, which he used as brush-cutters to reclaim old pasture grown back beyond his ability to keep up with the forest's steady encroachment. Now he runs thirty head on forty acres of rescued land, well fenced with three strands of barbed wire and—where temptations are strong—woven wire stock fencing. Between May and October his cattle require no daily labor. Only the calves are creep-fed good hay—allowed access through slatted openings too narrow to admit their mothers—until they are a year old. In winter, he feeds hay in various locations, dropping bales from a pickup truck in areas that have recently been cleared of trees, so that the resultant manure there will help establish a new stand of grass the following spring.

Henry Carse in Hinesburg, Vermont, runs forty-five registered Highlanders and a number of crossbreds. He prefers the Shorthorn cross, but has used Angus and Hereford as well. Last year he sold sixty-five sides of beef out of his locker to satisfied customers. Like Flynn, Carse sees the Highlander as a useful alternative for the small farmer with limited acreage, an alternative to such labor-intensive crops as truck farms or orchards.

In our own experience, the Highlander has proved to be an easy feeder. Our original plan was to graze the heifers in sections of pasture the horses had just vacated in hopes they would clean up the tougher grasses the horses disdain. It was also our expectation that this procedure would cut down on parasite infestation by keeping the grasses uniformly short and exposing the manure to sunlight. But the Highlanders prefer to browse along the fence line on blackberry bramble, burdock, staghorn sumac, poison ivy, tree leaves, and windfall apples and pears. Thus we have had to return to the rotary mower to clear out patches of tall grass.

The heifers have solved the garden glut, however. The massive, undiscovered cucumber or zucchini is a Highlander's delicacy. They have done away with a twenty-foot row of beet tops, followed by ten Chinese cabbages that had gone to seed. Late last fall they worked their way through eighty pounds of green tomatoes, devoured all the apple pomace from the annual sauce-making, and throughout the winter snacked happily on banana peels, grapefruit and orange rinds, and a dozen surplus pumpkins.

Given all its virtues, why has the Highland breed been so slow to gain acceptance? "Conservatism on the part of ag people," says Dr. Mark Wahlberg, extension specialist in animal science at Virginia Polytechnic Institute. "A man raises Herefords because his daddy and his granddaddy raised them. And the Highlander's exotic looks may scare some people off. A lot of folks are prejudiced against horns. Horns take up a lot of room at the feed trough and can get in the way in loading chutes. And, of course, accidents can happen. When a big fellow goes to chase a fly off his flank with the tip of his horn and you're standing in the way, you can get a good nick."

The trend in beef cattle is toward something bigger all the time; the Highlander is not an ideal feedlot animal. But, as Dan Flynn points out, "People don't stop to think that the bigger it is the more you have to feed it."

At present, only a handful of farmers are raising Highlanders or Highland crosses commercially. Many owners are hobbyists, not serious breeders, which creates difficulties for future generations, because the hobbyists are not breeding selectively to improve the foundation stock.

The oldest and biggest breeding farm in the Northeast, Pitcher Mountain Farm in Stoddard, New Hampshire, has for many years been the mainstay of the industry. So many of their cattle have gone to establish other herds in the area that breeders like Carse and Flynn have chosen to import bulls— from Scotland or Colorado—to broaden the gene pool.

Henry Carse feels that the breed does not thrive in warmer climates. He prefers not to sell his stock south of Massachusetts. He also believes that Highlanders do best at higher elevations.

But the main problem, most Highland enthusiasts agree, is lack of promotion. A wave of self-criticism washed over every breeder I talked to; the general consensus was that Highland people would have to get over the notion of using their association as a kind of private club.

It is amusing to think of these red, brindle, black, yellow, and white shaggies as a snob bovine. In fact they derive from the most basic blue-collar roots. Circumstantial evidence indicates that the breed descends from the bovines of central Asia. The long reddish hair, solid conformation and stocky legs are traits shared by the now-extinct auroch, the bison, yak, and musk ox of that region. In an essay published in the ASHBA quarterly, *The Bagpipe* (Spring 1980) Michael Fennell traces the hypothetical route they took northward from Tibet. He theorizes that primitive drovers moved the precursors of the Scotch Highland breed across the Tarim Basin and then easterly to the fertile grazing ground around the Black Sea. Following ancient trade routes, the cattle gradually were driven north into Scandinavia across the Danish peninsula. From there they island-hopped westward into the territory of Scotland. In support of this interesting thesis he offers some convincing evidence that links Highland and Shetland ponies to their ancestors in the Mongolian tarpan and the related Przewalksi's horse, all of which share, with bisons and yaks, the shoulder stripes associated with their central Asian origins.

In a climate not unlike northern Scotland's, though less forbidding than Tibet's, the Scotch Highlander stolidly munches its way across the northern United States and Canada. Facing into the wind and snow during a storm so that its long coat is blown flat rather than ruffled up, the Highlander endures and thrives. Perhaps, given the new trend away from grain-fed, feedlot-fattened animals, the Highlander is to become the backyard cow of tomorrow.

Journal—Late Winter— Spring 1978

13 February 1978 Today, in the dying butternut tree that holds up the clothesline from which depend various suets and the main sunflower-seed feeder, an owl. Peterson's indicates it is a barred owl, not an unusual bird in these surroundings. He arrived, like a poem, unannounced. He squatted on the branch, puffed to an almost perfect roundness against the cold. His gray and brown and buff markings imitate the landscape of tree branch and caterpillar nest tatters against the snow. I could not, as the cliché has it, believe my eyes at first, and tried to make him into some recognizable artifact of nature—a clump of windblown leaves, for example. Like the notes for a poem, he would not go away but merely swelled there passively all through breakfast.

The squirrels did not show themselves, wisely. The chickadees are fearless, or at least know they have nothing to fear. The blue jays likewise. I note that our narrow-faced, downside-traveling nuthatches were absent all day.

---

14 February The owl is a Cheshire cat of an owl, noise-lessly appearing, disappearing, flapping off soundlessly on immense wings, returning, higher up than before. He swivels his head almost 360 degrees, like a Japanese puppet-balloon held aloft on a stick. The face is infinitely old, infinitely wise, very catlike. When perched, no wings or claws are evident, lending him even more mystery than is warranted. Like the finished poem, he makes it all seem easy. Not since last winter's wild turkeys, not since last summer's swallow nestling sideshow on the front porch stringers, has there been better indoor viewing.

15 February This resident owl of ours, I muse on the third day of his tenure in the butternut, resembles nothing birdlike. Most of all he looks like a baseball pitcher in a tight spot, winding up, swiveling to check the runners at first and second, then . . . the balk. The old owls of my poems were of the furtive sort, night hooters. Whenever I did catch a daytime glimpse of them, they were in a hurry to get under cover and they seemed ragged, weary, diminished by a hard night's work. This one is larger than life-size. He has assumed the stature of a godhead in the birdfeeding zone, though today he and the squirrel eyed each other and nothing happened. Perhaps the owl is full of his nightly mice? I noticed that the squirrel took care, while cleaning up the spilled sunflower husks, not to turn his back on the owl. Although only a small red squirrel, perhaps he is too large to tempt even an enlarged owl.

20 February The filly these cold mornings canters in place in her stall. Too excited to tuck into her morning hay, she

wants desperately to be let out, to run off some of that ado-
lescent exuberance. Some days it is impossible to get a halter
on her before her morning run. Today I unleashed her early
and stood in the barn doorway to enjoy the aesthetics of her
romp. The young horse is so improbably gracefully made; the
body itself has not yet filled out, the legs are still dispropor-
tionately long. That extraordinarily high tail carriage, the whole
plume of it arched over her back, and the floating suspended
gait she displays at the trot, are inherited from her pure Arabian sire. It takes quite a lot of racing, dodging, cavorting,
and bucking to get the morning kinks out. She can come to
a dead stop from, say, thirty miles an hour. She can attain
that speed in, say, three strides. What she does is harsher
than ballet, and less controlled, something like dribbling down
a basketball court, feinting, shooting, wheeling, back to the
other end, and so on. The exultation I feel as I watch her
move so freely and with such euphoria is a kind of glorying in
effortlessness, no matter how much muscle is involved. She
moves the way a poem ought to move, once it's crafted.

24 February Putting in the spiles I lean on the brace and
bit, having to use all my weight to keep the metal spiral an-
gling upward into the tough tree. How astonishing, after the
hole is bored, that the sap glistens, quivers, begins to run freely.
To think that I have never seen or done this before! I am as
captivated as the city child finding out where milk comes from.

We have cobbled a Rube Goldberg sort of contraption
for boiling the sap down: an ancient kitchen sink for an evaporator, leftover bits of corrugated metal roofing to enclose the
fire, a rack and grill from a long-abandoned fireplace gadget
that was designed to throw heat back into the room but failed
to do so to an appreciable degree, and two rusty pieces of

stovepipe, one with a damper. Plus piles of trash wood, pine, primarily, which gives off too much pitch to be safe to burn indoors.

1 March   Although it is still too cold for any appreciable melt, one tree—we note that it's on higher ground than the others and thicker, too—is really running. The sap freezes almost as much as it drips, forming a great colorless cake of possibility. John Burroughs, quoted by the Nearings in their maple syrup text, says: "The first run, like first love, is always the best, always the fullest, always the sweetest."

How much still is dormant! And how the spirit yammers at the spirit hole, howling for spring to inch in. Now the horses are shedding, a gradual, indifferent sort of daily loss. Both Jack and the Boomer have grown an extra outer coat of coarse, short white guard hairs. These fly off in the slightest wind or are rubbed off, with grunts of horse pleasure, as they roll in the sun on the snow. Truffle, a mare of more refinement and considerable bloodlines, pure bay, has no such tough outer layer. Now that she is eight months pregnant she rolls only on one side, gets up, lies down anew to roll onto the other. Three months still to go. The foal will come at the end of May, in the full throat of spring.

Today I started half a dozen flats for the garden, of French celery and big-leaved basil, broccoli and cauliflower, and, optimistically because they always die of indoor wilt before it is time to set them out, some miniature hybrid tomatoes. Our bedroom is now crowded with trays hogging the available south light of two windows. Step stools, their step sides facing the windows, make ideal shelves on top of the counter that runs along the south wall. The secret is that I put some aged manure in the bottom of each tray. I hope it is sufficiently ancient so that it won't, at room temperature, begin to reek.

7 March The chickadees have changed their tune and are now singing their mating song. Those same beggars who perched on my arm in January while I was filling their feeder now stay away most of the morning. They are citizens of independent means.

11 March Everything is softening. The change, when it came, was direct, happened overnight. In spite of longing, reaching for it for weeks, we were still overtaken. The sap is running, a delightful chorus of plink-plinks in the sugarbush.* The horses are shedding apace. They itch enough to roll every morning now, all the guard hairs a drift of fuzz in the air, free to nesting birds for the taking.

The other night we did the barn chores together and stood a while enjoying Jack enjoying his hay. Wise old campaigner, he totes it by the mouthful to his water bucket and dunks as he crunches, not unlike the way our forebears crunched sugar lumps as they sucked up their tea. Soon the surface of Jack's water is a yellowish froth from the hayseeds. Alternately he sucks and chews, a moist rhythm.

13 March The morning one is convinced it is spring there is a rising, manic elation for having outlasted the winter, for having come through, in Conrad's phrase, unscathed, with no bones broken. Last evening at feeding time two crows

---

*In 1982, we converted to tubing.

went across the paddock cawing in midair, and I felt goose-bumps rising at the nape of my neck. That crows know when to return! That ice will melt, snow cover shrink, days lengthen! Nothing is to be taken for granted after a winter of below-zero mornings, ice frozen in all the water buckets, the horses' nostrils rimmed with ice. After north winds that scour and cleanse and punish. After nights so cold the house clapboards crack and whine. Now the bad times ebb. The split wood lasted, we shall even have a cord or so to spare, as a hedge toward next winter. We calculated correctly on the hay, we congratulate ourselves on its quality, none of it dusty or moldy, enough of it so we can be generous. And Truffle now swelling and swelling, retreating more into herself, less sociable, more self-protective. In a few more weeks we will separate her, almost nine months of her eleven-month gestation now over.

15 March Of mud, muck and mire. Of the first, *The American Heritage Dictionary* says: "wet, sticky soft earth." Mire is deep, slimy soil or mud whereas muck is (1) "a moist, sticky mixture, especially of mud and filth," or, (2) "moist animal dung mixed with decayed matter and used as a fertilizer." Ergo, manure. Then there's *to muck about,* British, a synonym for puttering. To *muck up* is to mismanage, and the usage most common in these parts, *to muck out,* synonymous with *to redd up,* make tidy or clean, to put in order, usually before company comes, probably, says *The American Heritage* again, from ridden, to rid. Of mud, muck and mire: they epitomize the general condition of the paddock at this season of steady, inexorable melt while our whole small world runs downhill, everything a rivulet.

The purest variety of mud squelches upward from the

bases of the maple trees from which it is now necessary to gather sap twice a day. I carry ten gallons uphill twice a day. Mucking out, I displace and wheel off two barrowloads at a cleaning, I estimate forty pounds worth. This does not count wielding the ice chopper each morning to free the sliding barn doors which are kept shut* to discourage further inflowing of melt. What we want is outflow. We chip channels through the frozen barn floor, a tundra of semipermafrost, sawdust bedding, hay sprinklings, and manure, and build a dam across the inside lip to coax and cajole a downward, outward flow of what must necessarily all turn to water by May.

Life is hard, it says between my shoulderblades.

Every day the sap gets hauled uphill from twenty taps to metal trash barrels set in the snow at a point where the land thinks better of it and levels off for a respite. The pioneers called these flat places "kiss-me-quicks," little plateaus where they could halt the team for a breather.

We boiled in our contraption for two windy days. It is sooty, cold, discouraging work, stoking and restoking the fire. At the end of each day we ladled the remaining four gallons into the canning kettle and set it indoors on the Jøtul overnight. Next morning I finished the syrup on the gas stove; it surpasses the fanciest grade triple-A boughten variety. Ours is even paler, purer, and has a buttery taste to it. We are full of grimy complacence. But what a lot of work! By rights maple syrup ought to cost five hundred dollars a gallon. Anything less is a swindle.

22 March   Statistics acquired at Saturday's all-day broodmare clinic run by the University of New Hampshire's exten-

---

*On grounds of poor pulmonary hygiene for the horses, we soon abandoned this practice.

sion service. The room was full of a hundred horse-proud people much like me. "Each stallion is a person," proclaimed the stud manager of Vermont's one Thoroughbred breeding farm. "The egg of the mare is about the size of a grain of sand, or one-two hundredth of an inch." She is born with approximately fifty thousand of them. A stallion will produce from seven to ten billion sperm per day. Five hundred million are sufficient for good fertilization. Exhaustion trials indicate that five or six mares per day are optimal, even for a young stud. The sperm is 1/2,000 of an inch in length. We saw many swimming about in slides projected on the screen.

"A mare," says the old-timey polo-playing vet, Stephen Roberts, "a mare is like a Vermonter: an animal that thinks otherwise."

A foal comes out into the air like a diver entering the water, in that position, front hooves on either side of cheek bones. The mare in labor can exert 170 pounds per square inch of pressure, so rotate a wrongly placed foal between contractions, otherwise you may get your arm broken. A lactating mare will yield up to 50 pounds of milk per day. The incidence of twinning is extremely rare, less than one percent of live births. Although twinning occurs in fifteen to twenty percent of conceptions, these almost invariably abort before the eighth month. Safe, viable births are rare with twins. One fetus ends up taking up most of the placental area. Even if she delivers two, the mare "hasn't the mentality," says Roberts, to take care of two and must be separated from them except at feeding time, for fear she'll step on one, sleep on one, forget one, and so on. Something new to worry about.

6 *April*   Of the Clivus Multrum and fruit flies, this note. The owners of Clivi Multra are not unlike Mercedes owners,

which is to say, obsessed with the special nature of their possession. My cousin by marriage, the Mercedes owner, feels for his car the same affection I feel for my animals. He respects, even honors his machine's idiosyncrasies. The keeper of the Clivus Multrum displays the same sort of bemused pride, but with more justification. These earth toilets, waterless, self-composting aerobic indoor privies, are the wave of the future, even though one New Hampshire town has vetoed the installation of any within its jurisdiction. Unquestionably, it is a better arrangement. Can one adjust after all these years of rigorous bathroom hygiene, years of the sound of the redemptive flush carrying off our wastes and gallons of precious water, to the silent slanting cavern of fiberglass? I am uneasy squatting there. Our friends' Clivus, an hour north of us in true sugarbush country, has been in operation over a year now. They claim, indeed boast of success with it. Then over martinis they confess, as the Mercedes cousin might to an unidentifiable squeak, confess to an infestation in the Clivus of fruit flies.

I have sent away this day for a five-month supply of stingless hymenoptera, small, bite-free wasps that prey on the larvae of most of our common flies, stable flies, face flies, house flies, and so on. Fruit flies are also mentioned in the prospectus. One sprinkles the monthly shipment upon the manure pile or on fresh manure in the pasture (or down the Clivus, I should think) and nature, urged on a little, does the rest.

28 April No peepers yet. The trees are still bare though the lilacs are budding. Daffodils in bloom yesterday, willow showing yellow shoots, forsythia still without color. Such a slow season! Or is it the annual impatience? Nothing much above ground in the pastures, but the horses are full of vinegar so they must be getting some vitamins from the browse.

Coming back home from a week in Salt Lake City where spring abounded, skies were blue and weather balmy, is, contrary to expectation, not a downer. The secret knowledge that I'm to have two springs buoys me. It's enough to make one accept the Resurrection in all its dogmatic regalia. If ferns can, if the wake robin trillium can, if the coprinus mushroom on the manure pile can flourish so showily, then He is risen.

Our visiting mare, Shandy Dancer, all 16½ dapple gray Thoroughbred hands of her, arrived last Wednesday in the rain. Much confusion and outrage at first. Gentle Truffle took considerable umbrage at being turned out with this stranger and would at first not allow the new mare closer than a strong stone's throw. Boomerang, unused to strangers, responded in two ways. First, she made her jaw-clacking, lips-pulled-back submission gesture, the one that says, I am but a suckling foal, do not harm me. Then, perplexed as to gender and in the throes of her first heat, she flagged (raised her tail) and squirted urine. Jackanapes, king that he is, although gelded, strutted, bucked, shook his mighty neck, and tossed his head. The fence between the two sections of pasture, much of it my own handiwork, has given way in a few places. The rails are hemlock, the posts range from twelve to fourteen feet apart, and the span is too great to take the strain of all the rubbernecking going on between two sets of horses. Every morning I go out with my galvanized nails, hammer, and some short pieces of hemlock for mending. It's now a pretty patchy, poor-mouth sort of fence, but it's holding.

This morning we were remembering when Jack first came to live with us and how he cowered, far from Elephant Child's hooves, meekly holding back till last by many lengths when the crew filed in for supper, or out of a morning. He knew his place in the pecking order. Now he is President for Life, a real banana republic–style dictator, and he keeps all the others in line. Oddly, he never kicks or nips Boomer. When he wants her to move on he pushes her forward with his lowered head, like a great hornless ox.

29 April   This last week of April, all those little lurchings toward spring have landed us smack in the middle of the season. Pine siskins, crossbills, evening grosbeaks are back. Robins, redwing blackbirds, and cowbirds are back. The indefatigable barn swallows are back, swooping and diving hard for the first insects. My flats of tomatoes are now hardening out on the porch; they look healthy enough to flourish in the earth in a few more weeks. The broccoli and cauliflower have been transplanted into the cold frame where they seem to be standing still, sulking. All my winter dill died while I was in Utah. But the parsley we kept as a house pet right through from October is bushy and strong and as of today is back out of doors. Early peas are going in today.

Some few blackflies are abroad, particularly in the pasture when the wind dies. Just enough to remind us of the incursion to come. Just enough to make me want to press on with planting before they peak.

15 May   Who can keep a journal past the first week of May? All in a one-day seizure, cattails, fiddlehead ferns, and nettles up for the picking. Nettle soup for supper. Three days later, marsh marigolds, which my neighbor Henry calls, as the British do, cowslips. The exquisite tedium of preparing the garden, plowing in last winter's manure, adding lime, de-stoning, smoothing with the patience if not the dexterity of frosting a cake. If you live with an engineer, you respectfully measure and line up your rows, keep a garden plan on graph paper and do your homework. Did I add half a day's labor to refurbish the fence of chicken wire, eight inches of which is buried to foil woodchucks, moles, voles, and mice? Meanwhile the air has filled with blackflies. Some days, if we dare to speak out of doors, we inhale them. Some days, like this one, a blessed breeze holds them hovering at bay.

May means grass, manna to the horses after a winter of hay. They set about browsing with ferocious intensity. The tonic of spring juices creates a considerable amount of whin-nying and squealing and racing, ruckus of the variety called horsing around. Everyone has lost his/her winter coat. The filly positively shines, like a simonized Jaguar. Truffle is pon-derous and grave, she walks as though her feet hurt and per-haps they do, as she totes that heavy unborn foal from day to day.

Fulsome bird life. The feeder overcrowded with rose-breasted grosbeaks, purple finches, and half a dozen gold-finches queued up on the clothesline awaiting an opportunity. The swallows are nesting. They made their usual slapdash repairs to the nests over the brick terrace and once the eggs are hatched will shriek alarm and dive-bomb me if I dare to exit through that door. My peas are up, tentatively. The onions seem off to a strong start.

The peepers were later this year than any year I can remember. They did not give voice until May 8 and only this week have they found their true range. Once they're in full swing, it is deafening to walk by the lower pond at sunset. It is the purest form of noise pollution.

◆◆◆

19 June I could not write this before today. It is three weeks since the morning I found Truffle's stillborn foal sprawled on its side in her stall, and Truffle lying quietly beside it, the placenta still trailing from her vagina. She had delivered it only moments before, a big, possibly too big, seal-brown filly, still warm to my touch, one eye glinting as if with life, the mouth slightly ajar so that its pink tongue, brilliantly pink in the graying five a.m. light, shone with the promise of life.

The vet came an hour later. He could find no cause but insisted it had never breathed. It had died either before or during its trip to the outside. I am not yet through blaming myself for not being there during Truffle's labor. She had shown no sign, no colostrum waxing on her teats, no restlessness the night before when at ten p.m. I made my final check of the barn. I remember that I felt her milk bag (for the hundredth time), felt her belly, and gave her a bit more hay. I go back and replay that day before, that evening before, I even replay the early dawn when I think now I heard a kick in the barn, a knock that might have been the portent. Had I dressed and gone to her stall then, had I waked fully and hurried out at that signal, we might have a healthy foal on the ground. These are the things I chew on, worrying them like the smooth gum space of an absent tooth.

We dug a grave behind the old chicken coop, dug and pickaxed and crowbarred away the stones, scooped and shoveled in a drench of early-morning, avid mosquitoes. Then we lifted the lovely heavy corpse into the wheelbarrow. The head lolled, hanging out, and I then cradled it and eased it back behind the rim of the barrow. I especially remember the little protective fuzz hairs that lined the ears, it was as perfectly made as that. We laid the foal in the earth and I got down beside it and folded the long legs in, tucking them back into fetal position, and then we shoveled the earth back over it and finally packed the top with stones so that nothing would disturb the grave.

It is already green there now.

A horse-friend from New York state writes me her condolences. She too has lost not one foal, but twin Thoroughbreds. "I would have spared you this shared experience if I could," she says. According to some astrological prognosticatory chart, we are both sixes on the scale. Sixes, Mary Beth writes, practice all their lives to die well, "act as Morticians of All Life and hold private burying rituals in their hearts."

So it is. So it has been. Truffle, two days later, was quite herself again. Her milk never came in, so she was spared the discomfort of a swollen udder. She never grieved. She licked the dead foal when I came into her stall that morning. She nudged it once or twice with her muzzle, and when it did not respond, simply turned away.

O to turn away.

Popple

Around the perimeter of every field, beggar trees en-croach. Gray birch and green poplar creep stealthily in, wrist bone-thick the first year, thighbone the next.

Popple is a soft word for poplar. Rolled over the tongue, it is said less in affection than in grudging acknowledgment of the tenacity of the species. Its usage is informal, says *The American Heritage Dictionary,* but the term is of ancient deriva-tion. While folk etymology has long connected *popple* with the Latin *populus,* for "people," it is actually rooted in the Latin *pōpulus,* which probably derived from the Greek *pteleya,* meaning "elm."

A next-to-useless wood, *popple.* Nothing that requires even heat can be cooked over a stove chock-a-block with poplar logs. Good for a quick hot blaze, the wood dies away almost before the biscuits are baked. Shingles are made hereabouts from the hefty midsections of mature popples. These shrink, drying, like un-Sanforized cotton. We know, having once shingled the exterior of a generator house with the local product. A year later the siding, gap-toothed and short-skirted, leered at all comers.

Still, any wood will burn. With all that idle popple at hand, of course you piece it out in the woodstove along with dependable ash and maple chunks. Even gray birch is better. It dries more easily, lasts a little longer. Popple seems never to dry out until it is debarked, or at least sharply scored clean around. On the theory that anything a horse will do a person need not, we scatter four-foot lengths of newly cut poplar in the pasture for our equines. All winter, the sounds of their gnawing on bark make a hauntingly hollow *thock!* at midday. Old-timers claim that poplar bark acts as a vermifuge or anthelmintic. Whether or not it acts on intestinal worms, it keeps our horses from attacking fence boards and corner posts in the boredom of the hard season. They seem to thrive on that occupational therapy and have become adroit at rolling the logs over—even in deep snow—to get at the fresh juices of the underside. As they polish off the bark, we stack the naked, fat towheads to dry along the fence line and entice our workers with new torsos and limbs to chew.

This cycle of horse and cellulose, field and popple, shuts down with the coming of the grasses. By the first of May the mares lose interest in woody fodder, disdainfully step over the last logs and mosey along, noses down, to catch the newest green sprouts as they emerge. All summer, behind their backs, the uncut poplars swell and prosper, getting ready for next winter, the winter after that, another, and another. Ineradicable popple going on after us suggests a comfortable kind of forever.

The Unhandselled Globe

Last week I saw two friends off on a backpack trip to Moosehead Lake in central Maine, there to paddle a fiberglass canoe for a week or so. They left, jaunty in their bright yellow Goretex jackets and matching pants, their nylon packs with Velcro fasteners on aluminum frames. Foam pads and sleeping bags were rigged sausage-style on top of the packs. Inside were freeze-dried dinners; magic powders for instant cooking fires; polypropylene socks to draw out the day's sweat from under their Nike sneakers; Deet insect repellent, used by the U.S. Army in Vietnam; a waterproof flashlight from L. L. Bean; a folding saw from Brookstone; a harmonica; and a paperback copy of Henry David Thoreau's *The Maine Woods*.

After they departed in their four-wheel-drive Subaru, I opened my copy of *The Maine Woods* to the appendix. Item VI, "Outfit for an Excursion," solemnly lists supplies for two men and their Indian guide setting out in July some 140 years ago: "a check shirt, stout old shoes, thick socks . . . one pair drawers . . . one blanket, best gray, seven feet long . . . veil and gloves and insect-wash . . . soft hardbread, twenty-eight pounds; pork, sixteen pounds; sugar, twelve pounds . . . six lemons, good to correct the pork and warm water. . . . Expense of preceding outfit is twenty-four dollars."

Nowhere is Thoreau's preoccupation with particulars more evident than in this wonderfully complete appendix, listing trees, plants, birds, quadrupeds, and Indian words in addition to the "Outfit for an Excursion." From the Indian glossary we learn that *Michigan* is the name of a "good-for-nothing fish"; *Alleqash* is the word for hemlock bark, useful in shaping tepees. The lake gained its name from the Indian hunting camps on its shore.

The literal is always Thoreau's base. Just as he surveys Walden Pond with cod line and stone to eradicate the myth of its bottomlessness, so in this heady account of the spell the Maine woods cast over him he constructs a terminology of measurement and specificity with which to plumb the wilderness.

"I speak only of what I saw," he says by way of introduction to his list of more than a hundred flowers, plants and shrubs, citing both their Latin and popular names. Nothing escapes his attention. In a clearing he notes such recognizable species as dandelion, lamb's-quarters, shepherd's purse and buttercup, commonly thought of as having been introduced from Europe, and speculates that they may have "accompanied man as far into the woods as Chesuncook, and had naturalized themselves there. . . ."

The list of quadrupeds is small, and includes the moose— "*wood-eaters,* the word is said to mean." Thoreau was enchanted to discover that the Abenakis had separate words not only for the male and the female, but also for "the bone which is in the middle of the heart of the moose (!), and for his left hind-leg."

It always makes me a little sad to remember that after all the care he took with this text, Thoreau did not live to see it in print. When he died of tuberculosis in 1862 at the age of forty-four, he was still revising the essays, "a knot," he told Ellery Channing, "I cannot untie." In fact, the last sentence he spoke was said to contain only two intelligible words, *moose* and *Indian*.

Moose and Indian abound in this book, composed of three essays drawn from three forays Thoreau made into the northern wilderness. He first traveled there in 1846, while he was living in the little hut on Walden Pond and recording in his journal the reflections and daily events that were to make his reputation as a natural historian and philosopher.

The chief purpose of the first trip was to climb Katahdin—Ktaadn, he spelled it then, "an Indian word, signifying highest land." Only four recorded ascents predate Thoreau's. From the sound of it, his was a daring venture: he climbed for long stretches over the tops of old spruce trees that had grown up between huge glacial boulders.

> Once, slumping through, I looked down ten feet, into a dark and cavernous region, and saw the stem of a spruce, on whose top I stood, as on a mass of coarse basketwork, fully nine inches in diameter at the ground. These holes were bears' dens, and the bears were even then at home.

In *Walden* Thoreau can speak of "the friendship of the seasons" and claim that "every little pine needle . . . swelled with sympathy and befriended me." But in *The Maine Woods* he must cope with a wilderness so savage and so profound that it seems to have burst the bonds of historical time. Here, he stands "deep within the hostile ranks of clouds . . . a dark, damp crag to the right or left," and compares his situation to that of Prometheus on his rock. The scenery is "vast, Titanic,

[151]

and such as man never inhabits." He is hard put to deal with the isolation: "Some part of the beholder, even some vital part, seems to escape through the loose grating of his ribs. . . . He is more lone than you can imagine."

More lone—not the sojourner in Concord, but a frightened mortal on the flanks of Katahdin. "Nature has got him at disadvantage, . . . pilfers him of some of his divine faculty. . . . She seems to say sternly, why came ye here before your time?"

In 1853 he went north again, this time to Chesuncook Lake, and in 1857 he made the major circle of the Allagash and the East Branch of the Penobscot with Joe Polis, his Indian guide.

Emerson complained about Thoreau's endless fascination with the wilderness, confiding to his journal (these transcendentalists were staunch diary-keepers) that "Henry . . . talks birch-bark to all comers"; but I revel in the sonority of Thoreau's response to the extremely rugged climb up, then down, Katahdin, most of which he accomplished by himself, as his companions stayed behind to make camp.

> I looked with awe at the ground I trod on, to see what the Powers had made there, the form and fashion and material of their work. This was that Earth of which we have heard, made out of Chaos and Old Night. Here was no man's garden, but the unhandselled globe. It was not lawn, nor pasture, nor mead, nor woodland, nor lea, nor arable, nor waste-land. It was the fresh and natural surface of the planet Earth, as it was made for ever and ever,—to be the dwelling of man, we say—so Nature made it, and man may use it if he can.

The search for that unhandselled globe is what has driven climbers to Everest, homesteaders to Alaska, explorers to the source of the Amazon. The concept of the unhandselled globe now applies to outer space, which seems made purely out of Chaos and Old Night; however, it lacks its resident lyricist, at least so far. None of the voyagers to the moon thought to feel "pilfered of divine faculty." Has technology robbed us of our capacity for awe?

To his own townspeople Thoreau was a radical and an eccentric, a man without a vocation, supporting himself doing odd jobs, devoting himself to what seemed to them inconsequential rambles, and living like a hermit on the shores of Walden Pond. What he did best was to observe, gauge, record, and measure every aspect of nature, reporting his findings in more than twenty journals, from which his published work is drawn. And wherever he went, his sympathy for the animal struggle for survival went with him.

At the sight of a slaughtered moose, in this instance a female separated from her nursing calf and gunned down, he wrote: "a tragical business it was . . . to see the warm milk stream from the rent udder, and the ghastly naked red carcass appearing from within its seemly robe, which was made to *hide* it." In fact Thoreau was never quite comfortable with the ethos of hunting. Indeed, even casting for fish gave him some disquiet. "I cannot fish without falling a little in self-respect," he says in *Walden*.

"This hunting of the moose merely for the satisfaction of killing him," he continues in *The Maine Woods*, "not even for the sake of his hide, without making an extraordinary exertion or running any risk yourself, is too much like going out by night to some woodside pasture and shooting your neighbor's horses."

[153]

An aroused Thoreau, the angry conservationist, is at his rhetorical best condemning the loggers' depredations. Much of *The Maine Woods* examines the logging industry in the middle of the nineteenth century and its effect on what we have learned to call the ecology of the region.

Speaking of "the chopper," Thoreau says that "he admires the log, the carcass or corpse, more than the tree. . . . The Anglo American can indeed cut down and grub up all this waving forest and make a stump speech and vote for Buchanan on its ruins, but he cannot converse with the spirit of the tree he fells—he cannot read the poetry and mythology which retire as he advances."

This is a taste of the Yankee asperity Thoreau brings so often to bear in the service of goodness and truth as he conceives them. He is rather more ambivalent about the American Indian, wanting desperately to see in him a noble savage who might have stepped out of the pages of Fenimore Cooper. But the Indian who might impart great revelation to the effete, civilized white settler is merely a myth. The romantic image of purity and quiet strength evanesces before the reality of the native American already greatly corrupted by the white man's liquor, the white man's diseases, his guns and ammunition.

Alas, Thoreau's Indians are unwashed and untidy, lacking the good middle-class virtues of the man of Concord. They have lost the knowledge of their forebears, lack a sense of their own history, and are illiterate. Absent, too, is the great fortitude he expected of them. At one point, his Indian guide "lay groaning under his canoe on the bank, looking very woebegone, yet it was only a common case of colic. You would not have thought, if you had seen him lying about thus, that he was the proprietor of so many acres in that neighborhood. . . . It seemed to me that, like the Irish, he made a greater ado about his sickness than a Yankee does, and was more alarmed about himself."

But Thoreau's Indian is at home in the forest; he can strike out cross-country, secure in his ability to come out of the woods unharmed at the exact place he entered. The white man is at a loss in the bush; he does not dare to leave his campsite after dark:

> You commonly make your camp just at sundown, and are collecting wood, getting your supper, or pitching your tent while the shades of night are gathering around and adding to the already dense gloom of the forest. . . . you may run down to the shore for a dipper of water, and get a clearer view for a short distance up or down the stream. . . . That is as if you had been to town or civilized parts. But there is no sauntering off to see the country, and ten or fifteen rods seems a great way from your companions, and you come back with the air of a much travelled man, as from a long journey, with adventures to relate, though you may have heard the crackling of the fire all the while,—and at a hundred rods you might be lost past recovery, and have to camp out.

I treasure this description of the dense evergreen forests of the Northeast, for they remain our precious resource. Yet how many of us have actually gone deep enough into the woods so that no extraneous sound—no truck or barking dog, chainsaw or human speech—penetrates? There "the trees are a *standing* night, and every fir and spruce which you fell is a plume plucked from night's raven wing," rhapsodizes Thoreau. He is entitled to his hyperbolic metaphor, for he has been there. And then immediately he shaves the sentimentality of his raven's wing with a description of the lengths to which

[155]

one must go to deter the mosquito hordes, ever a recurrent theme.

Remoteness is less threatening in this century. With crampons and pitons and nylon ropes, with emergency oxygen and two-way radios, we can assault the highest peaks. But although our wild places have shrunk, all of us who write, however tangentially, about the human place in nature hold a legacy from Thoreau. His language of specificity, from its soaring allusions to mythology to its startling metaphors, goes beyond the clinical measurements of the laboratory biologist, with whom he shares a passion for accuracy. Thoreau makes us see ourselves as part of the picture, standing somewhere in the middle ground, looking in both directions, to the mountains, and into the moss at our feet.

A Sense of Place

I have too many horses. It is not reasonable to stuff the barn with so many of all ages: the two yearling fillies, the three-year-old colt who will carry me, I hope, into old age, the two broodmares, bred again for April foals, and the hundred-mile competitive trail horse, who was our firstborn.

How can you be a poet? I ask myself in the bitter February dawn, stomping out in my felt-lined L. L. Bean boots, feeling my nose hairs freeze in the first ten seconds of exposure to the shocking air of twenty below zero. The horses are icicle-bearded, watchful, intolerant as hungry children. They pace and nicker as I measure out their flakes of hay, mixed timothy and brome and clover that we put up last June, and after the hay, sweet feed—a mix of grains and molasses that has, alas! congealed into clumps that must be pried apart with a tool. I use an aluminum sweat scraper, an apt irony at this season. First I feed hay to the little Arab mare who paws while she waits. Not that I want to reward a bad habit, but she is digging a ditch in her stall, and besides, horses are notorious imitators. I must hurry before one of the others catches on or we will have an orchestra of excavations. "Hay first, water next, grain last," as the poem has it. I clomp back up from the paddock to the main barn, lower two jerry cans of hot water from the insulated laundry room down through the hay trapdoor, trot back down to the stall area and thaw the ice in their buckets. After that, I enter each stall with the proper allotment of grain, the broodmares' with a sprinkle of vitamins on top.

Did I forget anything? The barn cats never show themselves at the morning feed once the temperature plunges. They're curled up like armadillos in the chinks between hay bales stored above. The indoor dog pretends he's still asleep on the ancient sofa in the back hall as I come in. He waits for the new zeal of the woodstoves, now that I've restoked them, before he importunes me for his breakfast. The bird feeders were refilled last evening, at dusk, after their patrons had gone to roost. No lambs to tend to; they went to slaughter in November. A moment of stasis as the coffee makes ready. Time to reflect.

Not Thoreauvian time—time is but the stream I go afishing in—or, with the lilt of exhortation, there is more to day than dawn, but alert time, newly awakened, newly certain of another harsh day in this "month of the hard palate," as I have called it—thinking, reappraising time.

It's madness, this glut of critters to look after, but it is a glut of shared needs. They need me as custodian of their confined lives, and I need them in a variety of ways—aesthetic, maternal, and some inchoate, perhaps indecipherable ways, all bound up in this matter of influence—influence of region, place, idea.

I cannot imagine myself living, as a writer, outside New

England. When I am away from the farm, locked up in motels or hotels into which no outside air may come without the intervention of machinery; when I am on the road for poe-biz and must eat Styrofoam airline breakfasts and cardboard airline lunches, I can stand back from this life and raise up some comments about it. What Louise Bogan called "subliminal mewings, roarings, and retchings, on odd scraps of paper" come out of these forays into the world, falling often onto the backs of boarding passes. Eventually these jottings may work out as poems on my desk in my study, a narrow little upstairs room that looks out onto the winding dirt road below.

Nor is it quite true that I cannot write away from home. Of course I can. I have on occasion written fiercely fast and even immodestly well when put on hold in a distant county, a poet-in-residence, for instance, in Pennsylvania or Maryland or Florida. I can, in fact, see my place, my hardscrabble kingdom on a hill, more clearly from a distance. I have forgotten in what anonymous motel, in a brown room smelling of old cigars, I wrote the first draft of the following poem. I know that it was winter and I was acutely, guiltily homesick and the overwhelming helpless admission of our own mortality visited me there. I know too that a New England winter is the very archetype of winters, and that winter itself signifies in the Jungian scheme of things, in the collective unconscious, the final phase, the end of sentience. So the poem conscripts all its forces to outlast the season.

Feeding Time

Sunset. I pull on
parka, boots, mittens, hat,

[159]

cross the road to the paddock.
Cat comes,
the skinny, feral tom
who took us on last fall.
Horses are waiting.
Each enters his box
in the order they've all
agreed on, behind my back.
Cat supervises from the molding cove.
Hay first. Water next. Grain last.
Check thermometer: seven degrees.
Check latches. Leave.

The sky
goes purple, blotched with red.
Feed dog next.
I recross the road to the woodshed.
Snappish moment with cat
but no real contest.
Wag, wag, kerchunk! The plate
is polished. Dog
grovels his desire
to go inside, lie like a log
by the fire.

Two above.
Above, it's gray
with meager afterglow.
Feed birds next.
I wade by way
of footprint wells through deep snow
to cylinders on trees.

A Sense of Place

Cat follows
observing distribution
of sunflower seeds.
Checks out each heel-toe
I've stepped in, in case
something he needs,
something small and foolish lurks.
No luck.

Penultimate,
cats gets
enormous supper:
chicken gizzards! Attacks
these like a cougar
tearing, but not in haste.
Retires to barn loft
to sleep in the hay,
or pretends to. Maybe
he catches dessert this way.

Now us,
Dear One. My soup, your bread
in old blue bowls that have withstood
thirty years of slicings and soppings.
Where are the children
who ate their way through helpings
of cereals and stews
to designs of horse, pig,
sheep on view
at the bottom of the dish?
Crying, *when I grow up,*
children have got their wish.

It's ten below.
The house dozes.
The attic stringers cough.
Time that blows on the kettle's rim
waits to carry us off.

Clearly, the impulse for poems is here for me, in the
vivid turn of the seasons, in the dailiness of growing things,
in the quite primitive satisfaction of putting up vegetables
and fruits, gathering wild nuts and mushrooms, raising meat
for the table, collecting sap for sweetening. Without religious
faith and without the sense of primal certitude that faith
brings, I must take my only comfort from the natural order of
things.

The sense of place underwritten by private history is part
of that natural order. An elderly neighbor stumps up the hill
to visit. His daddy and his granddaddy before him were born
in this farmhouse and tended the cows on the place all their
lives. There were cows named Mary and Grace and Easter
Lily and his grandsire and father and he himself in his boyhood
led them back to the barn by lantern light in winter, creeping
down the slickensides of granite outcroppings through snow
fog in the late March thaws. By that same lantern light they
rescued new calves their mothers had hidden behind hummocks or down in the swales, nor was it an easy task to carry
a weak newborn half a mile through the slurry of thickly rained-
on old snow. And many the night he sat by the woodstove
with an ordinary glass bottle full of cow milk with a rubber
nipple, working on a weakling to get it "up enough" to put it
back with the mother. There is no way of course for me to

assess what kind of animal husbandry these old-timers practiced. Just because it was yesteryear I don't want to be deceived into thinking they were paragons of virtue. I try to resist my old neighbor as his reminiscences take on proportions heroic as Beowulf.

The stamp of time, the continuity of memory unbroken converge as we tour the reclaimed pasturage. He points out where the blueberries came sweetest. He nods recognition of that stand of red pine planted by the CCC in 1938 to be harvested in twenty years for telephone poles, and then left to overgrow, rot and reseed themselves in a jumble. But our sojourn hallows the ground, if you will allow that highblown an interpretation. It is a poor ground, gravelly glacial till that has to be teased along with lime and fertilizer every other year. A winter's worth of stored manure and wood ash are flung over it in spring.

When I was a child growing up in Germantown, Pennsylvania, lawns were a desirable commodity. More than that, the condition of a lawn bespoke the degree of thrift, consideration, cleanliness and moral fiber of the householder. None is so poor he need sit on a pumpkin, Thoreau remarked; no house was so genteelly shabby that it need harbor crabgrass or dandelions in its small sward. But what my eye wants here in this minimal clearing in the Mink Hills is an expanse of fields.

It has taken us twenty years to achieve these fourteen fenced and barbered acres of meadow grass rescued from the two-hundred-odd craggy acres we own. Regularly we mow the weeds, mullein and thistle that the birds sow, clip back the encroached-upon edges where birch and popple and wild cherry creep, break up manure clumps, and pursue the errant milkweed by hand, before it can set pods. Even so, once the first frost comes, the only areas where the grass still thrives are the small plot over the septic tank and the reserved-for-people strip that surrounds the farmhouse.

What I long for, after Labor Day, is just one more big pasture, ungrazed on, mowed to a luscious four-inch carpet, a virgin field to carry our six horses into late autumn. Every year I mourn as we lock them out of one two-acre enclave after another, in order to permit the good tough brome and clover a chance to consolidate before the eroding rains of November. Every year I make small unkeepable vows to have another section of woodland cleared, stumped, bog-harrowed, limed, fertilized and seeded. Every year reason and economics prevail.

It isn't the easy limestone bluegrass spreads of Kentucky and Tennessee that I have in mind. The Puritan in me wants these hard-won upland fields, their humps and spines running out to the hedgerows. When I look left or right, I yearn for pastures with daisies and black-eyed Susans, hawkweed and Indian paintbrush visible at the far edges. Fields someone has paid attention to. The terrain is too hilly for mechanized equipment except for our ancient Gravely walk-behind rotary mower and the jackhammer-heavy weed whacker. It is the surprise of clearings come upon in the midst of tangled, second-growth forest. These New England upland pastures are like a secret garden, like the impulse toward a poem. Every dip and scarp is engraved now on my brainpan. *My* fields, my old neighbor's fields, his forefather's fields. How like Kurtz I have become, exclaiming, *my ivory!*

The evanescence of this life tied to the land, the eating away by time and technology of our last links to the earth, to the cycles of growth and decay, the contemporary repudiation of manual labor and menial daily chores are realities that grieve me. How many more years will there be horses silhouetted against the top line of fields in early twilight? How much longer will the mixed hardwoods and conifers that stand all along the perimeters of the fields, an ever-shifting palette of textures and shades of green, catch fire in fall before thinning down to the cold essential of the pines and hemlocks that stay on? How many more explosions of goldfinches, a bird so common hereabouts in midsummer that we call them New England canaries, flying up like lost petals of some exotic yellow flower?

Increasingly I think that we are doomed transients here. There is not one full-time farmer left in my community. Those who carry on the old traditions, raising pigs or sheep or cattle, keeping hens or quail, or a few geese for old times' sake, tending the few fertile fields that they will hay in season, now do so on a part-time basis, holding down outside jobs as sawyers in the local mill or traveling out of town to the light industries that have sprung up everywhere. Agribusiness has made it impossible to sustain a family any longer, for example, on a herd of thirty Holsteins.

What will become of that not-quite-vanished system of values that lingers in the New England countryside, abetted by the harshness of the climate and the exigencies imposed by isolation? I don't want to write elegies to vanishing virtues nor do I wish to mythologize the remaining stalwarts. But I cannot be blind to the miniature fortitude of humans pitted against the vagaries of the weather. In June or July the thunderheads roll in; the hay must be gotten under cover before the storm breaks. Sap, once the full spring run begins, must be boiled down into syrup continuously or it will spoil. At the sugarhouse three families take turns spending the night to stoke the fire under the evaporator. In order to shelter the animals, the new barn must go up before snowfall.

A few years back, an old barn across town that housed

twenty horses and two thousand bales of new hay was struck by lightning during a wicked August storm. Luckily, all but two of the animals were rescued, but the structure and the hay were a total loss. It was a family farm. Insurance did not begin to cover replacement costs.

Remember memorizing "Sweet are the uses of adversity"? Short of finding books in the running brooks or sermons in stones, it was nevertheless instructive to see how many local people volunteered their time and skills to get a new barn up before the weather closed in. Weekends and late afternoons a crew swarmed over the post-and-beam skeleton. There was nothing heroic about it—just the steady whack of hammer on nails, the high-pitched whine of the table saw as the roof went on, siding went up, windows appeared, stalls were roughed out. My small tithing was two days of creosoting stalls, a job I loathe at home and am at pains to avoid.

Not everybody chipped in. Not all motives were pristine and neighborly, I am sure. But it was impressive to see the old Yankee spirit that manual labor shared is manual labor soon over, and that this homely act reinforced our identity with place and with the austerity of nature.

Except for the occasional marginally successful cheesemaking or horse-training farm, this individualized way of life has become an anachronism. No matter that some of us still run a hundred taps in March or raise a dozen feeder lambs from spring till fall or keep a cow or some goats. No matter that a few of us still breed our mares to the best available stallions and raise new foals spring after spring, comparing their bloodlines. We are insignificant. In the government jargon of the day, we don't impact anything. New England now is little more than a nostalgia trip for people in urban centers to make every autumn, to admire the colors, to celebrate the season with apples and cider from roadside farms, and artful displays of corn shocks.

Wendell Berry, a farmer-poet from Kentucky, has devoted most of his life to explaining that good farming is not just another industry, like the manufacture of automobiles or transistors. "The reasons," he says, "are complicated but they may be summed up in two facts: first, farming depends upon living creatures and biological processes, whereas the materials of industry are not alive and the processes are mechanical; and second, a factory is, and is expected to be, temporary, whereas a farm, if well farmed, will last forever—and if poorly farmed, will be destroyed forever."*

Agribusiness today is an easy target. We know what the broadscale use of insecticides and herbicides, what the heavy, mechanized reliance on industrial fertilizers is doing to the land and to the consumer. Factory methods of animal husbandry are both inhumane and counterproductive as antibiotic-resistant organisms enter the food chain from cattle fattened on Terramycin, hens on Aureomycin, pigs on triple sulfa. I will try not to rail here against the cruelly confining conditions under which much of America's livestock is raised today. Nor do I want to eulogize the vanishing virtues of the small farmer, whose lambs and pigs and heifers were turned out unmedicated on pasture and whose chickens scratched in real dirt every day. Without magnifying the family farmer into a Paul Bunyan, we can at least observe that he rotated his crops, of necessity allowing one or more fields to lie fallow each year; that he understood the connection between overgrazing and parasite infestation. If he threw winter rye or buckwheat seed on his plowed land in the fall, he understood that green man-

*New York Times, Feb. 26, 1985, p. 27.

ure tilled in is cheaper than 10–10–10. A stable population of farm families meant, until recently in our history, that another generation would be around to carry on. That the wisdom would be handed down, the skills not lost or forgotten. Most of all it meant that human beings still felt some connection to and responsibility for the animal lives and the land in their keeping.

Are these emotions proper to poetry? I think so. Where there are questions of survival, the poet belongs on the battlements. Of course the largest question is the threat of nuclear obliteration, but surely the extermination of the family farmer is not the smallest. If we lose our place in life, we will also lose our ability to respond in humane and significant ways to our surroundings. If I am to write poems constructed from words arranged in their natural word order in the conversational tone of voice used between consenting adults, I need the centrality of the natural world to draw on.

The animals are my confederates. They arrive, sometimes with speaking parts, in my dreams. They are rudimentary and untiring and changeless, where we are sophisticated, weary, fickle. They make me better than I am, as I said in an old poem. Also, they rescue the past. They are the Golliwogs, the Would-be-goods of my childhood. Guileless, predictable, they help define who I am.

I am especially lucky because my daily life provides a metaphor for my work, allowing me instant access at all times, crosshatching reality with the snail tracks of the unconscious, enabling me to pull poems up out of the well of the commonplace. It is a paradox, living in isolation in the country—it is making the world over as you want it to be, while at the same time coexisting with nature. The domesticity of our situation, the nest seen from inside as against the broad scale of physical forces outside: hard freeze, blizzard, rain, extreme heat and drought—yields certain proprietary rewards. Digging your own fence post holes, building your own run-in shed provide a sense of order in chaos, however briefly attained. Perhaps dealing sequentially with extremes of heat and cold teach forbearance. Blackflies besiege us in May, mosquitoes arrive in June, deerflies torment any flesh in the woods or along the perimeter all summer long. In winter we must shovel snow off two shed roofs after every appreciable storm, to say nothing of digging out house and barn. Hay and water have to be hauled by hand up to the broodmares wintering in the hilly pasture above the house. And so accustomed have they become to warm drinking water that they bang their buckets against the fence rails to announce their desires.

The nature of some chores changes when water freezes, and again in the spring when the thaw becomes reliable, but the chores themselves are a constant. Mucking out, for example, is eternal, and takes place in any weather. An astute student recently pointed out to me the prevalence of rain and snow in my poems. I realized with a start how right she was; bad-weather days are my most likely writing days.

Growing most of your own food, you come to appreciate how labor-intensive it is, and how it doesn't count when it's your labor. Once you have become accustomed to fresh vegetables cooked to order, once you have roasted your own organically raised lamb, baked foodstuffs using your own maple syrup, the synthetic products of the marketplace lose their appeal. I have become a terrible snob about restaurants, for example.

Yet I do not want to overstate the autonomy this lifestyle confers. Where would we be up here on our hill without the internal-combustion engine, the salt, flour, toilet paper, jug wine of the grocery store down in the village?

Nor does the solitary rural life provide "peace of mind,"

an opiate once very much in vogue. There is no more, no less peace of mind in the disciplined life of the barnyard than there is in the routine of the office. Despite Yeats's romantic yearning for Innisfree "where peace comes dropping slow," I would have to say anxiety lurks inside every decision that has to be made on the farm day by day just as it must in an urban setting. And why is peace of mind a goal at all? Whatever peace of mind is out there comes as a side effect of doing other things, says the old Hebraic Puritan inside me, equating tranquillity with hard physical labor. I think of Housman: "Up, lad! When the journey's over / there'll be time enough for sleep."

In a poem one can use the sense of place as an anchor for larger concerns, as a link between narrow details and global realities. Location is where we start from. Landscape provides our first geography, the turn of the seasons our archetypes for our own mortality. In the following poem, a great many warring notions coalesced for me when I was able to put them all inside the confines of that forty-by-forty vegetable patch.

After the Harvest

Pulling the garden I always think
of starving to death, of how it would be to get by
on what the hard frost left untouched
at the end of the world: a penance of kale,
jerusalem artichokes, brussels sprouts,
some serviceberries, windfall apples
and the dubious bounty of hickory nuts.

A Sense of Place

Pretty slim pickings for the Tribulation
if that's what this is, preceding
the Rapture I choose to be left out of.
Having never acceded to an initial coming
I hold out no hope for a second
let alone this bland vision of mail-order angels
lifting born-again drivers up from behind the wheel
leaving the rest of us loose on the highways
to play out a rudderless dodgem.

When parents were gods survival was a game
I played in my head, reading by flashlight
under the covers *Swiss Family Robinson*
and *The Adventures of Perrine,* who lived in a hut
and was happy weaving moccasins out of marsh grass.

I longed to be orphaned like her, out on my own
befriending little creatures of the woods
never cold or wet or hungry. To be snug
in spite of the world's world is the child-hermit's plan.
Meekly I ate the detested liver and lima beans.

Now all of the gods agree, no part of the main
can survive the nuclear night. And yet
like a student of mine who is writing a book
on an island linked by once-a-week ferry
to Juneau, where one pay phone and a hot springs bath
suffice for all, in innocent ways we still
need to test the fringe of the freezing dark.
He thinks he can be happy there year round
and the child in me envies his Cave of the Winds.

Meanwhile I fling cornstalks and cucumber
pea and squash vines across the fence
and the horses mosey over to beg carrot tops.
I am mesmerized by the gesture, handfeeding
feathery greens to the broodmares. This could

be last year or five years or ten years ago
and I sense it is ending, this cycle of saving
and sprouting: a houseful of seedlings in March,
the cutworms of May, June's ubiquitous weeds,
the long August drought peppered with grasshoppers

even as I lop the last purple cabbage, big
as a baby's head, big as my grandson's brain
who on the other side of the world is naming
a surfeit of tropical fruits in five-tone Thai.
A child I long to see again
growing up in a land where thousands, displaced
unwanted, diseased, are awash in despair.

Who will put the wafer of survival on their tongues
lift them out of the camps, restore
their villages, replant their fields, those gardens
that want to bear twelve months of the year?
Who gets Rapture?

Sidelong we catch film clips of the Tribulation
but nobody wants to measure the breadth and length
of the firestorms that lurk in Overkill
certitude of result through overwhelming strength
they define it in military circles

their flyboys swirling up in sunset contrails.
The local kids suit up to bob for apples
go trick-or-treating on both sides of Main.
November rattles its dry husks down the food chain
on this peaceable island at the top of the hill.

Is this an anywhere in the North Temperate Zone poem?
Possibly. Would my work be significantly different if I lived
in Illinois or Oregon? Am I provincially a New Englander, a
Yankee, with the extra-deep taproot of a transplant?

I think yes. The quality of detachment, of skepticism,
the understated wry response to good fortune and to ill, the
respect accorded individual eccentricity, even the harsh insis-
tence on a man's inalienable right to use or abuse his property,
his animals, according to his own lights, all seem particularly
if not peculiarly regional. Best of all the New England poets,
Robert Frost captured this mixed essence of Samaritan and
curmudgeon.

During my poetry-formative years, however, I remember
that Frost was dismissed as a somewhat acerbic cracker-barrel
philosopher who spoke with an upcountry accent. Not until
the early fifties was his poetry taken seriously by those responsible for establishing the canon. The turning point for me
came with Randall Jarrell's essay, "To the Laodiceans," in which
the critic asks rhetorically, "What other poet, long before we
had begun to perfect the means of altogether doing away with
humanity, had taken as an obsessive subject the wiping-out of
man, his replacement by the nature out of which he arose?"*

Like that earlier ardent conservationist, Thoreau, Frost

*Randall Jarrell, *Poetry and the Age,* Knopf, 1953, p. 39.

[173]

was totally committed to his point of view—not always a flattering one as regards the human species—and could, in the most casual way, employing a colloquial idiom, bring aspects of the natural world into sharp focus. I suppose I was further enchanted by Frost's unswerving stand on the principles of his selfhood. In a letter to a friend, Frost wrote: "Anything I ever thought I still think. Any poet I ever liked I still like. It is noticeable, I go back on no one. It is merely that others go back on me. I take nothing back. I don't even grow. My favorite theory is that we are given this speed swifter than any stream of light time or water for the sole purpose of standing still like a water beetle in any stream of light time or water off any shore we please."*

Although that last statement will not bear close scrutiny given the almost perpetual motion of the water beetle, it says something about the adamantine character of the poet, a trait that is highly visible in Thoreau as well.

For as many years as I can remember, Henry David Thoreau has been my special mentor. The landscape I walk is his. I visit his trees, inspect his snowstorms, seek out his moose. The epigraph for a collection of my poems, *The Long Approach,* is taken from a diary entry in Thoreau's *The Maine Woods.* His transports of hyperbole, whether in the service of polemic or praise, always create a little shiver of empathy in me. A writer full of inconsistencies, he disarmingly acknowledges his mood swings. One of my earliest published poems tried to explore this duality. "My quotable friend," I called him; "my quotable friend, so kneed and knived / by students extracting the metaphor. . . ."

I reread *Walden* every year or two. Largely I do so for

---

*Cited in James M. Cox's introduction to *Robert Frost, A Collection of Critical Essays,* Prentice-Hall, 1962, p. 13.

the refreshment of his aphoristic style, but partly I succumb to nostalgia. When I was a young instructor at Tufts University, all of us junior faculty taught *Walden* in lockstep; it was part of the core curriculum in freshman English, along with a Shakespearean tragedy and the Sermon on the Mount. We were required to give a common three-hour final exam, made up in good part of multiple-choice questions based on the text. With much hilarity and black humor we sat around the table and invented absurd alternatives for the multiple choices. "In his statement, 'The gross feeder is man in a larva state,' Thoreau advocates: a) polyandry; b) fasting; c) more fastidious housekeeping; d) vegetarianism; e) gluttony."

Lately, I find myself returning to *The Maine Woods* for its exalted sense of place. Climbing Katahdin, Thoreau was a man nervously balanced on the lip of the unknown, half in exaltation, half in dread. Something of that primitivism is available to us still every day in our own second-growth woodlands. And the more highly programmed a person is for asphalt, sirens, buses and traffic lights, the more susceptible he or she is to the assaults of silence and space that take over, a hundred yards from house or barn. Where I live, it is so quiet at night that the hooting of an owl habitually wakes me. I can hear a horse cough, the cats trap their nightly mole or mouse, and the first faint traceries of rain beginning. Visitors frequently complain that they cannot sleep. Their eyelids are pinned open by the quiet, by the absence of human activity.

If Thoreau made legitimate for me a holy sense of the minute observable details of the natural world, another New England poet encouraged and abetted me in my early years as a poet. John Holmes, a professor at Tufts University, befriended many of us. His house in Medford, his bourbon and Doris Holmes's fish chowder supplied the easy hospitality that brought such poets as Frost and Ransom back to refresh themselves after their public readings, where we could adulate and interrogate them. In the late fifties we formed a workshop— Anne Sexton, George Starbuck, Sam Albert, Holmes and Kumin—and met every other week in one another's homes to try out and plead for our new poems. John's was the most overtly New England voice, Frostian yet meditative in a more discursive way. We were mercilessly critical of each other but endlessly supportive as well. Whole books came out of those jagged and frequently dramatic work sessions. Starbuck's *Bone Thoughts*, Sexton's *To Bedlam and Part Way Back*, Holmes's *The Fortune Teller*, and my own *Halfway* all took on their essential outlines during that period.

Sexton's influence on my work—and mine on hers—is now a matter of public record. Certainly as women writers who began to accrete poems before the Movement, we shared many of the same concerns. We were suburban housewives and mothers. As poets we took a respectful backseat to the male poets. We did not talk about our husbands and children in public; that would have been gauche indeed. We were flattered to be told that we did not sound like the little three-name Violet Letitia ladies. Our rebellion was underground and mannerly, but discontent was jiggling our elbows. As one another's most immediate and sympathetic audience, I suppose it was inevitable that we take on some of the same subjects. But I like to think that our voices are distinctively separate, even as critics shuffle our poems today in search of overlapping images.

Actually, I think the most significant influence on my own work was the impact of W. H. Auden's tetrameter line, combining thing and thought in what were to me astonishing new ways. He was the poet I imitated; his was the metrical control I worked for. My models were male simply because there were so few women poets to provide working examples. Bishop and Moore distanced themselves in their highly individuated ways—Bishop by a kind of severe classical purity into which no self-referential *moi* might intrude, and Moore by her own quirky encyclopedic outreach into the realm of mythic creatures and foreign artifacts. They were adrogynous poets. Louise Bogan at that time had been little read or anthologized, though she had much to teach. Rukeyser was a distant and muffled voice. Millay, Wylie, Amy Lowell, H. D. were treated dismissively, beneath notice. Of course there was always Emily Dickinson to reach back to, long and safely dead—an Emily ill understood and still largely disparaged by the male critics of the fifties and sixties as a writer of tiny enigmatic versicles.

It is a much better time to be a woman poet now. It is a harsher world as well. Is there something gender-specific about a woman writer's sense of place? To the extent that women are now writing about female relationships, mother-daughter bondings and rivalries, the high tide of feeling running between sisters, the answer has to be yes. This is a territory that was for the most part a vast terra incognita only fifty years ago. Now we are seeing these interior landscapes of feeling, touched and colored by the outside setting, in new ways.

I think my own work has grown bolder, more overtly political and certainly more despairing over the past decade. The private concerns, the particulars that still enlist my interest are much the same, but the context in which I see them has broadened. I dislike abstraction in poetry. I dislike the overdetermined, self-congratulatory, deliberate obfuscation that I feel is the hallmark of a certain academic school of letters. For the most part I prefer not to write poems about paintings, sculptures, musical compositions and the like, thinking that to give in to the impulse to embellish another's art diminishes rather than enhances it. This is a Calvinist sort of purism and I have broken my own rule from time to time. With Bogan, I believe that the proper purview of the poet is to deal in some way "with the terrible, unaccountable processes of the human spirit."*

In this increasingly complex era I think the poet's obligation has also been enlarged. Now I must face the issues of survival, of hunger and genocide, of natural (or unnatural) human depravity. Nemerov says, in an essay called "The Muse's Interest," "the whole business of poetry is vision, and the substance of this vision is the articulating of possibilities still unknown, the concentrating what is diffuse, the bringing forth what is in darkness."

To run ahead in the darkness, to hold to a vision of what is true and unshakable seems to me the poet's immutable role in the culture. Certainly mass media have diluted our regional differences. Today, at least on television, we are a blandly one-accent nation. In a poem, I said:

> *Affirming my past, our past in*
> *a nation losing its memory, turning*
> *its battlegrounds into parking lots,*
> *slicking its regional differences over*
> *with video games, substituting outer*
> *space for history, I mourn*
> *the type-O, any-deaths of Mecca,*
> *Athens, Babylon, Rome,*
> *Radford, country towns*
> *of middleclass hopes and tall corn . . .*

*Elizabeth Frank, *Louise Bogan*, p. 371.

A Sense of Place

But it is not nostalgia that drives the poem. The energy comes
from saving alive some of "the past that breaks out in our
hearts," as Rilke put it. A sense of region is surely part of
that process.

The Long Approach

In the eel-thin belly of the Metro Swearingen
banking in late afternoon over Boston Harbor
the islands eleven lily pads, my life loose as a frog's
I try to decipher the meaning of hope rising up again
making music in me all the way from Scranton
where the slag heaps stand like sentries shot dead
at their posts. Hope rising up in my Saab hatchback
one hundred thousand honest miles on it as I speed
due north from LaBell's cut-rate autopark
to my spiny hillside farm in New Hampshire.

March 21st. Snow still laces the manure heap
and flurries lace the horses' ample rumps
but in here it's Stephen Foster coming back to me
unexpurgated, guileless, all by heart.
Tis summer, the darkies are gay, we sang in Miss Dupree's
fifth grade in a suburb that I fled long ago.
Gone are my friends from the cotton fields away
to—an allusion that escaped me—a better land I know.
O the melancholia as I too longed to depart.
Now I belt out Massa's in de cold cold ground
and all the darkies are a'weepin on route I-93
but what I think of are the french-pastel mornings
daylit at five in my own hills in June when I may

[179]

leap up naked, happy, with no more premonition
than the mother of the Pope had. How the same
old pump of joy restarts for me, going home!

What I understand from travel is how luck
hangs in the lefthand lane fifteen miles
over the limit and no cop, no drunk, no ice slick.
Only the lightweight ghosts of racist lyrics
soaring from my throat in common time.

Last week leaving Orlando in a steep climb
my seatmate told me flying horses must be loaded
facing the tail of the plane so they may brace
themselves at takeoff. Otherwise you run
the risk they'll panic, pitch over backwards,
smash their hocks. Landing, said the groom,
there is little we can do for them except
pray for calm winds and ask the pilot
to make a long approach.

O brace me, my groom. Pray for calm winds.
Carry me back safely where the snow stands deep in March.
I'm going home the old way with a light hand on the reins
making the long approach.